W9-DIG-233

CRITICAL ACCLAIM FOR TRAVELERS' TALES

"This is travel writing at its glorious best."

—*Chicago Tribune*

"The Travelers' Tales series is altogether remarkable."
—Jan Morris, author of *Trieste and the Meaning of Nowhere*

"For the thoughtful traveler, these books are invaluable."
—Pico Iyer, author of *The Global Soul*

"Nightstand reading of the first order."

—*Los Angeles Times*

"…the popular Travelers' Tales collections offer a perfect fit for just about anyone, with themes of geography, women's travel, and a passel of special-interest titles on topics including shopping, pets, diners, and toilets around the world."

—*Chicago Sun-Times*

"These well-edited anthologies of first-person travel narratives are like mosaics: Each piece may add only a single note of color, but combine them and step back, and a rich and multifaceted portrait emerges."
—*San Francisco Chronicle*

"The Travelers' Tales series should become required reading for anyone visiting a foreign country who wants to truly step off the tourist track and experience another culture, another place, firsthand."

—*St. Petersburg Times*

"This is the stuff that memories can be duplicated from."

—*Foreign Service Journal*

TRAVELERS' TALES

3ºDAYS
— IN —
ITALY

TRAVELERS' TALES

3⁰DAYS
— IN —
ITALY

TRUE STORIES OF ESCAPE
TO THE GOOD LIFE

EDITED BY JAMES O'REILLY,
LARRY HABEGGER,
AND SEAN O'REILLY

TRAVELERS' TALES
PALO ALTO

Travelers' Tales and Travelers' Tales Guides are
trademarks of Travelers' Tales, Inc.

Credits and copyright notices for the individual articles in
this collection are given starting on page 199.

We have made every effort to trace the ownership of all
copyrighted material and to secure permission from copyright holders.
In the event of any question arising as to the ownership of any material,
we will be pleased to make the necessary correction in future printings.
Contact Travelers' Tales, Inc.,
853 Alma Street, Palo Alto, California, 94301. www.travelerstales.com

Art Direction: Stefan Gutermuth
Cover Photographs: ©Blaine Harrington
Interior design and page layout: Melanie Haage

Distributed by: Publishers Group West,
1700 Fourth Street, Berkeley, California 94710.

LIBRARY OF CONGRESS CATALOGING-IN-PUBLICATION DATA
30 days in Italy : true stories of escape to the good life / edited by
James O'Reilly, Larry Habegger, and Sean O'Reilly. --1st ed.
    p.   cm. --(Travelers' tales)
  Includes index.
  ISBN-13: 978-1-93261-42-1 (pbk.)
  ISBN-10: 1-932361-42-1
 1. Italy--Description and travel. I. OReilly, James 1953-
  II. Habegger, Larry. III. O'Reilly, Sean. IV. Title: Thirty days
  in Italy.
DG430.2A15 2006
914.504'93--dc22   2006020916

First Edition
Printed in the United States
10 9 8 7 6 5 4 3 2 1

Open my heart and you shall see
Graven inside of it — Italy.

—LORD BYRON

TABLE OF CONTENTS

INTRODUCTION

ITALY IS A CULTURAL HOMELAND FOR ALL OF US IN THE Western world, even if we are not Italian or of Italian descent. Whether you've never been there, or trod Etruscan and Roman soil many times, Italy is a place of a lifetime. No guidebook can quite reveal its secrets, no television documentary the charms of its wily and sensual people, no Fellini the fevered pulse of its life. You have to discover these things for yourself. But in the meantime, stories from travelers can help you shape your own memories-to-be, your Italian legacy of the future. In that spirit we've gathered here thirty writers to tell you what they discovered on their last trip.

If you had thirty days to spend in Italy what would you do? The simple fact is that there are so many things to experience in Italy that thirty days would but scratch the surface and launch you into planning your return. Nonetheless, the question remains: What would you do? Would you visit Assisi and walk the byways of Saint Francis or spend your time studying the antiquities of Rome? Would you wander Venice, Florence, or Trieste, or all three, and would you do it in the winter or the spring? Perhaps the energy and fashion sense of the Milanese interest you or the magnificent wine-producing regions that have their earliest origins in Roman times. Or you might wish to walk the old Roman stones of the Appian Way or try out winter sports in the Italian Alps. How about hiking the cliffs of Cinque Terre or taking a drive down the boot of Italy for some rough and tumble in Naples, a visit to Pompeii, or a hop across the Strait of Messina to Palermo enroute to the Egadi Islands, or a beach trip to Capri or Sardinia or the Italian Riviera? Or you might consider exploring the remote villages and hill towns of Basilicata and Puglia and Calabria and the Marche.

But no matter what one does in Italy—and among those choices will be so many memorable meals they will begin to blur—sooner or later the traveler is borne by gravity toward Rome, that ultimate locus of history that still reverberates with the echo of empire. Perhaps you will walk among the ruins of the Forum or the Palatine Hill, one of the seven hills of Rome, where emperors and history were made and unmade. In his splendid travel classic, *A Traveller in Rome*, H.V. Morton notes that the word "palace" is derived from the mansions that were built on this hill in Roman times. And that the Capitoline Hill, from whence our word "Capitol" is derived, was once the site of the greatest temple of the Romans—the Temple of Jupiter Capitolinus. The legend is that when the grounds were being excavated for the temple (around 600 B.C.) a human head was found, said to be that of the mythical hero Tollius. The soothsayers interpreted it as a sign that Rome was to become the head (*caput*) of the world and so the hill was called "*a capite Toli*." Another word in everyday use in those times came from the nearby temple of Zeus's wife, Juno Moneta. As the temple was also a mint, the word "moneta" comes to us down the ages as the familiar word "money." Likewise, the Papal Succession of the Catholic Church is the last living link with the Roman world and the papal line descends directly from the time of Tiberius, who was the Emperor of the Gospels. This is the only such institution directly related to Roman times still existing in the world.

The Roman model of government found its way into the U.S. Constitution with whole words like "senator" and "republican" being reused, such was the admiration of the Founding Fathers for Roman governance. The twentieth-century dictator Mussolini also sought to emulate the greatness of the Romans. He personally directed the draining of Lake Nemi in the Alban Hills outside Rome so that the stupendous pleasure barges of Caligula might be salvaged. These barges of immense size came complete with indoor plumbing, statuary, and heated floors. When the plumbing artifacts were examined, some of the valves were so modern looking that they were thought to be forgeries. (Alas, the pleasure boats were destroyed by retreating German troops in World War II.)

You might think that so much history would make Italians more nostalgic for past greatness but it seems to have had the opposite effect. Italians are so sure of their history, so familiar with it that it is hardly worth reflecting on—it is part of their common legacy and now their largess, their gift to the world. Enjoy their insouciance, their intolerance for the 9-to-5 routine, and their disdain for what we think of as order.

Live a little, carve out your niche, and turn whatever time you have in Italy into your own private cornucopia of days.

—The Editors

PHIL THOMPSON

BURGLARS IN PARADISE

It takes more than a key for this caper.

EVEN IF ONE SOMEHOW TIRES OF THE DAVID, GETS BORED with Pompeii, or yawns at the thought of another gondola ride, doesn't the prospect of renting a farmhouse in the Italian countryside still excite? Of course it does. It's every traveler's fantasy, and with a minimum of planning it can be the best vacation of your life. But do pay attention to the details. You've been warned.

A few years ago my family and friends rented a 200-year-old farmhouse in Umbria for a week. We drove all day from Florence in two tiny Fiats and an asthmatic diesel Peugeot. When we finally turned off the spur road and bounced along the rutted dirt driveway to catch our first glimpse of the house, we knew we'd gotten our money's worth. The house spilled down the hill in tumbled layers of rough-hewn stone and ended at a broad flagstone patio perched high above a misty valley. Surrounding the house was a shaggy meadow dotted with flowering weeds that rolled down the hill in a wave of green and yellow before dashing itself against a low rock wall at the foot of the property. A wobbly fence of ancient timber posts and rusting barbed wire surrounded the sides of the little compound, keeping a restless flock of sheep from entering and devouring the little flower garden beside the house.

Road weary but delighted at what we'd found, we set about unloading the bags of food and wine from the cars for our sunset feast while my wife went to fetch the key. The owners had e-mailed us the location of the key hidden beneath a loose rock in the belly of the ancient stone pizza oven built into the side of the house, the Umbrian equivalent of hiding the key under the mat.

He had been glowing with joy ever since the plane had touched down in Milan, and his radiance had only seemed to increase with the missing key.

We could hear the muted bells around the sheep's necks as they roamed about testing the perimeter fence, grazing dejectedly outside when it held. The sun was already low in the west, and the air had grown crisp and cool on that late fall afternoon. We could smell wood smoke from a farm nearby. It was impossibly beautiful, the precise reason why so many tourists are drawn to the Italian countryside, why whole fantasies are created around that "someday" trip to Tuscany or Umbria. This was it, the dream, right here, Eden without the snake. I took a deep breath of Italian October afternoon and exhaled, smiling, as my wife walked quietly toward me from the house.

"I can't find the key."

My smile froze. She was trying hard not to look like a woman who'd dragged her parents and friends halfway around the world and down miles of twisting country roads in order to make them shiver on an Italian hillside beside a locked stone farmhouse surrounded by ravenous sheep. She shook her head quickly, anticipating my obvious question.

"*Yes*, I looked everywhere in the oven, and *no*, I couldn't find it." Her lips were tight, tension glittering in her eyes. She looked over at her parents, now removing cubic yards of heavy luggage from the car. "But maybe *you* could find it." The optimism in her words didn't agree with the hard set of her face, but hope was hope, so I made my way over to the narrow arched opening to the pizza oven and looked inside. I couldn't see any loose stones in the floor of it but I wedged myself into the opening anyway. Feet waving in midair, I carefully fondled every inch of the floor, then let myself back down. Covered with soot and dust from head to waist, I raised my hands helplessly. There was indeed no key.

Word spread rapidly among our companions, and they gathered in a fidgety semicircle around the oven. Everyone was well past the days when an impromptu camping trip on a wet, dewy meadow or in a cramped European economy car would be considered a lark. "Well, I guess we'd better call Marta," my wife said.

Marta was a local woman employed by the house's owners to take care of the place. We'd been given her number in case of emergencies. With the sun sinking fast and the air cooling rapidly we voted unanimously that this qualified as an emergency of the first order. My wife took charge, gathering her mother and Linda, the third woman on the trip, to go with her to the nearest town in hopes of finding a pay phone. They revved up one of the Fiats and sped down the driveway, pausing only to latch the gate behind them to detour the opportunistic sheep. Then they disappeared down the road in a cloud of dust.

I said that we had voted unanimously that being locked out

of our vacation home in the middle of nowhere qualified as an emergency, but the vote had actually been 5 to 1. Our abstention was at that moment over by a shuttered window picking at the gap between the wooden shutter and the stone wall with a corkscrew, holding a sloshing glass of wine in his other hand. On the porch next to him was a freshly opened bottle of Chianti Classico and two more full glasses beside it. "There's gotta be a way we can get in here," said my father-in-law Dan, "but it'll be more fun finding it if we have a little vino first, eh? *Salute!*"

Dan has a well-deserved reputation for being grace-under-fire personified, immensely charming and levelheaded, particularly when he's holding wine, but on this trip there was an added dimension. Both his parents were Italian, his father born there before emigrating to the United States, and this trip to Umbria was a homecoming of sorts for him. He had been glowing with joy every since the plane had touched down in Milan, and his radiance had only seemed to increase with the missing key. He took deep breaths of the fragrant air and gestured around him dramatically. "Isn't this great?" he asked, rhetorically. Our companion Roger and I found ourselves agreeing, why, yes, this *was* great, and the three of us toasted the deepening sunset from the chilly porch of the locked cottage and felt, well, *great* about our prospects.

Newly fortified, we inspected the house's defenses more carefully. Dan had discovered that the shutters, while made of solid oak over an inch thick, left promising gaps between the wood and the irregular surface of the rough-hewn stone walls. Peering through the openings, we could see that the shutters were separated from the windows and doors they protected by the thickness of the stone, leaving a space of about six inches. Only the front door shutters had an external lock on them, so we deduced that all the others must be latched from the inside. If we only had a tool to use to reach down through a gap and into the darkness of the space inside, we might be able to throw the latch from the outside and get at one of the windows or doors. And, so our thinking went, if the shutters had been latched, might not someone have forgotten to lock one or more of the windows, or even a door, allowing us to just waltz right in and make ourselves belatedly at home?

A farmhouse in the country, even one that has been gentrified as a summer retreat for urbanites, has all manner of forgotten junk lying about in piles. Tangled nests of twisted wire and other metal objects fetched up in drifts at the perimeter fences, quietly melting back into the ground. Searching for anything that might serve as a tool, I kicked at the turf consuming one of those piles and found a thick piece of corroded iron strap about two feet long that could be bent with some effort into a long hook. Dan had located the most promising target, a narrow shuttered door at the far end of the house with a decent gap at the top. Dipping into the opening with my homemade hook, I felt around and found what seemed to be a little knob on the inside; I could just reach it with about an inch to spare. Pulling up didn't budge it, so, after an anxious moment where I almost dropped the hook into oblivion, I pushed down on it and the latch suddenly gave way. The shutters swung open to reveal that the inner door had not only been left unlocked, it hadn't even been closed. Dan flicked on the light switch. We were now staring into the house itself.

Oh, sweet victory! We high-fived and toasted each other anew, flush with pride. We had done it, we had broken into...

"The laundry room," said Dan. He shrugged his shoulders and took a sip of wine while we pushed past him to confirm. It was indeed the laundry room, with a little half-bath just visible beyond the washer and dryer. It was the work of only a moment to discover what Dan already knew: there was no connection from this utility area to the main house. We were still locked out.

"Well, the good news is that we now have a bathroom." I hoped I sounded more optimistic than I felt.

"No, gentlemen, the good news is that this isn't just the laundry room or a bathroom," said Dan, pointing into the corner. "The good news is that it's also the tool shed." There, on top of a workbench wedged into the small space, was an open toolbox overflowing with wrenches, screwdrivers, and even a pry bar. "To Plan B!" cried Dan, raising his glass again.

We had noticed earlier that the shutters' hinges were attached to the wood with regular screws that could be simply unscrewed, a security breach we had been unable to exploit earlier because the only tool we'd had at hand was Dan's corkscrew. Now, however, the laundry room had yielded up a heavy-duty ratcheting screwdriver, the next best thing to the key itself; we were back in business. We chose a window close to the front door that would be relatively easy to climb through, and proceeded to the attack. Pounding on each screw to loosen it, Dan muscled them all out with the ratchet, and as the last one slipped out I pulled the shutter free, exposing the window beneath. Rubbing his hands together with the relish of a successful safecracker, Dan confidently pushed on the newly exposed window. It wouldn't budge, securely locked from the inside.

"I don't suppose we have a Plan C," asked Roger, plopping himself down on the steps.

"What on *earth* are you doing?!!" my wife shrieked. We had been so focused on our efforts that we failed to hear the car return. We would-be burglars stood frozen in place, the severed shutter from the house askew in my hands, a handful of screws and the screwdriver in Dan's. Two empty bottles of wine lay at Roger's feet.

"Any luck?" I asked innocently. My wife shook her head as if she couldn't believe what she was seeing. "No, well, we did find a pay phone and a place to buy a phone card, but the line was busy and we came back to see if you had found the key and...and what on *earth* are you *doing*?"

"The good news is that we have a bathroom," said Roger helpfully, pointing to the open laundry room door.

The three women stood with their mouths open in shock and their arms tightly crossed while I explained ourselves as best I could. My wife shook her head slowly. "Well, I have to go back and try Marta again," she said, "but you *have* to stop dismantling the house in case someone comes by. She climbed back into the car with her mother. "Look for the key, maybe we missed it." Turning to the third woman, she said, "Linda, you stay and make sure they don't rip off any more shutters!" Off they went down the dusty driveway again, leaving our new babysitter to keep us in line.

No sooner had the Fiat disappeared down the drive than Linda whipped around and said, "Don't just stand there drinking, pour me a glass and get to work on more shutters!" Clearly Linda was the kind of babysitter you revered as a child, the kind who would let you drink beer and watch R-rated movies on cable. Dan clapped his hands together and set to work on opening another bottle, and I attacked another window. This time the work went more quickly, but the result was the same: the window within was locked. "Well, try the door," suggested Dan, ever cheerful.

"Maybe they got lazy. Those shutters lock, so why would they lock things twice?" With the sun touching the trees on the horizon and a serious chill to the air, his logic sounded impeccable, so we went to work on the door. Five minutes later, we pulled one shutter free and set it aside. Dan squeezed into the opening and tried the door. It opened.

We peered into the gloom at the shadowy forms of furniture and a fireplace; the archeologist who first looked inside King Tut's tomb and saw the glint of gold could not have been any happier than we were to see that huge stone hearth. We all squeezed inside, the room still warm from the lingering effects of the afternoon sun. We took a moment to toast our successful burglary, and then got to work. While the others brought all the food and luggage inside, Dan and I quickly reattached all the shutters and put away the tools. By the time my wife and her mother had returned from their second unsuccessful call to Marta, all the shutters were open, the house was flooded with light, and the four burglars were lounging on the patio watching the last of the sun disappear below the horizon. "You found the key!" they cried, greatly relieved. Dan smiled and poured his wife and daughter a glass. "*Salute!*" he said happily, and left it at that.

Phil Thompson is a native Californian with a lifelong addiction to living out of a suitcase. His wife is half-Italian, and he's spent the better part of their marriage drinking vino rosso *in a futile attempt to catch up. He lived in Tokyo for a time, during which he believes he was the tallest non-athlete in Japan. He once bowed to physicist Stephen Hawking on the banks of the Thames, and has waved to the Queen of England; more importantly, she waved back. Phil has a degree in Ecosystems Analysis from UCLA, and is currently a graduate student in Liberal Arts at Stanford University. He travels as often as he can, and writes from his home in San Mateo, California.*

2

CONSTANCE HALE

CUTOUTS

The night once had a thousand eyes.

ON NIGHTS WHEN THERE WAS A MOON, ALDO AND I WOULD leave Poggio al Grillo without a lamp. It wasn't hard to pick our way down the dirt road, and anyway Aldo knew its twists and turns by heart.

Some nights we walked as far as Vito Lippini's. There we might see, through a door cut into the stucco walls of an outbuilding, the family's *nonna* sitting on a stool in a golden rectangle of light, wearing a black dress and headscarf, as silent as Whistler's mother, staring down the vat of red wine. Some nights we would run into Ernst, the Swiss farmer, on his bicycle, hurrying home to his wife and children from a tryst with the Englishman's wife. Other nights we stopped in on Nino, who came from Milan only on weekends and brought his mistress with him.

Only a month earlier, it was me whom Aldo had stopped in on. I had just finished dinner and was cleaning up when I heard a deep voice outside. *"Cosa succede qui? Chi abita in questa casa scura?* (What's happening here? Who has turned on the lights in the dark house?) I opened the door to find a tall, fit man with gray hair, black eyebrows, and a neat, gray beard, accompanied by a silent German shepherd.

(Upon hearing that I would be traveling in Italy, a Milanese couple—friends from a theater class in Berkeley—had given me their country place in Tuscany for the fall. They hadn't warned me of this ad hoc night patrol.)

"*Sono amica degli Riccardi,*" I heard myself blurt out. "*Non parlo italiano.*"

"*Benissimo!*" the man replied. "I leeved two years in Feelahdellfee-ah."

> On another night, I learned that those same townspeople had taken to calling me *la regazza molto in gamba.*

And so we became friends: the twenty-six-year-old American girl, feeling very alone in a sprawling house in the Tuscan hills, and the fifty-six-year-old painter from Milan with his dog Doc. It didn't take long before we were eating dinner together every night.

After dinner we would walk, leaving the red traces of our wineglasses to seep into the new beech table ("It is too new, too perfect," Aldo complained) and leaving dishes to soak in the sink ("*l'acqua calda soltanto nella mattina*"; no hot water till morning.) Often we didn't stop in on anyone. We just wandered.

On a night when there was just a sliver of a moon, I was taught an Italian children's rhyme:

Gobba a ponente,

Luna crescente;

Gobba a levante,

Luna calante.

In Tuscany, apparently, the man in the moon was a hunchback. If his *gobba* protruded to west, the moon was swelling; if his *gobba* protruded to the east, the moon was diminishing.

On another night, I fantasized about the people of the town, Castagneto Carducci, imagining them as giant blue nudes. Aldo was going on and on about how they were "cut out," their isolation leading not just to poverty but also to provincial pettiness. Only later did I realize that he was translating *tagliati fuori* a bit too literally: he meant "cut off," not "cut out." His mistranslation took me to Matisse and the cutouts that the aging artist made in his last years in Provence. It didn't matter to me that these hills were a palette of ochre, umber, sage, and sienna; that night I imagined the townspeople as cobalt cutouts against an all-white background.

On another night, I learned that those same townspeople had taken to calling me *la ragazza molto in gamba*. "What did they mean," I asked, "that I had big thighs?" Aldo laughed. To be very much "in one's legs," he explained, was to show pluck.

This must have come in one of our conversations about my writing. At the time, I dreamed of becoming a writer; I scribbled in a journal and suffered from dark self-doubt. I didn't have a clue as to how to "become" an artist. I had not so much as tasted the kind of success he took for granted. He, after all, was a renowned painter. His studio at Poggio al Grillo (Cricket Knoll) included not just his own landscapes and nudes, but also a Warhol lithograph of Marisa Berenson, a Magritte, and a Picasso—all acquired in trades with other Italian artists. Aldo even prided himself on having once wittily put De Chirico in his place.

"What could you understand," I jabbed defensively, "about my predicament?"

"Ah," he consoled. "I know too tenderly the swing of the pendulum. One day: I am a genius! The next: I am a nothing."

I never called him my lover. It's not that we didn't share a bed—in this case, a modernish wood frame of his design that firmly held two independent twin mattresses together. It's just that that term failed to describe what I found in Aldo. It was as though I had met the person I would have been if I had been born exactly one generation earlier, and in Italy, and a man.

Aldo had the nerve to live ideas I was only beginning to flirt with.

He had never doubted that he was an artist. Not that he didn't take risks: He had grown up in a bourgeois Milanese family and had forsaken the family legacy for a deeply nonconformist life. He was still a Communist, long after that party had gone out of favor. He had never married. As a young man, he had fled to Philadelphia when he found himself hopelessly in love with his brother Cesare's wife. The exile didn't work; Aldo returned to Italy and helped his sister-in-law raise his niece and nephew. The relationship with his sister-in-law eventually foundered, but he stayed close to his brother's children: During the fall I was with him, he was fretting over the niece's husband, a heroin addict, and giving the nephew his half of La Gallinella, a stone house he owned with Cesare. (In the kind of symmetrical justice only possible in Italy, by this time the cuckholded Cesare was living in town with a former consort of Aldo's.)

The subject of freedom—creative, sexual, political—dominated many of our walks. Aldo was militantly opposed to many things. Like monogamy. Like complacency. Like violence. In the bedroom, a small ragged window was set into the wall beside the bed. Aldo had built the stone house by hand, and during a hiatus in the building project, a spider had spun a web in the valley between two stones. Aldo couldn't bear to destroy the web, so he placed a glass behind the spider and kept building. From the bed, you could stare through the web window, over several ridges covered with olive trees, to the Mediterranean beyond.

One day over lunch, I noticed a very thin steel wire that extended horizontally over my head, from one wall of Aldo's house to the other. Thinking it might be for hanging underwear on a rainy day, I asked about it. "After I built the house," he explained, ever the *maestro*, "I realized that there should be a beam there, for aesthetic reasons. The wire represents the beam."

Despite the aesthetic attractions of his house, I maintained my own quarters at the Riccardis'. I would go there during the day to write, and to play with arrangements of the paintings Aldo kept bequeathing me. They were all watercolors featuring the hills and the sea, or lithographs of black-ink nudes on bright white paper. As I moved them from bedroom to living room, from the seats of chairs to ledges built into the walls, I examined them for flaws. For imperfection, Aldo insisted, was the soul of art. To him, a perfect painting was merely decorative. A bit of watercolor out of control—or the self-doubt I couldn't escape—suggested Truth, Life, the Human Condition.

On nights when there was no moon, not even a *gobba*, Aldo would grab the huge Panasonic lantern that stood sentry next to the front door. We would follow the beam of the massive flash-light down the gravel drive, watch as it animated the pocks in the dirt road, feel ourselves cradled in a roofless room as the light picked up dusty banks cut into certain curves. I'd be transported to the dark courtyard of an ancient villa, or to the eerie majesty of San Galgano—the ruin of a Cistercian abbey in the Val di Merse whose ceiling and windows had long ago been carried off by the wind, whose walls enclosed a grand abbey now consecrated only to Space.

On one particularly dark night, shortly before I was to leave Aldo, in search of my own truths, the beam stretched indefinitely ahead as we fell uncharacteristically quiet, each lost in thought. Suddenly, in that tenantless night, there rose a porcelain-like tinkle. Aldo jerked the lamp 90 degrees, into the black emptiness.

There to our right, frozen in the beam and almost near enough to touch, was a flock of sheep. Hundreds of pairs of eyes glazed red-gold. All of us—the flock, the painter, the lamb of a writer—all of us stood frozen for a few eternal seconds. The wonder! Then one sheep turned its head, sharp hooves made the bone-dry grass rustle, and, in a symphony of bells, they were gone.

Constance Hale is the author of Wired Style *and* Sin *and* Syntax. *As a journalist she has written about Latin plurals and Internet clichés. She has also covered national politics, digital culture, and the spread of hula on the U.S. mainland. She lives in Oakland, California, and Hale'iwa, Hawai'i.*

3

BONNIE SMETTS

ONLY FISH

If only life were always so simple.

Each Italian travel morning as I head off to see the shinbone of a saint or a (now bloodless) Renaissance anatomy theater, my husband crisscrosses the street in front of me like a hound on a scent. I hold back as he disappears into backdoors of restaurant kitchens or reads menus posted out front. My husband is a chef, and he's in search of what food people call the *vibe*. I wait for the magic words, "That's it. We'll come back here tonight." Those words mean my husband is happy to accompany me the rest of the day.

One rainy week in a small Italian beach town with a single pizzeria, the balance between my husband's hunger for extraordinary dining and my insatiable appetite for the bizarre tipped precariously to my side.

Jeff would have protested a visit to the church I spotted at the summit above the beach but any destination was an excuse to be in the heated car. We found the narrow lane leading into the backcountry and climbed up away from the sea. Halfway to the top, Jeff suddenly stopped, "Go in and make a reservation." No kitchen check, no menu review, only a faded sign with a ship's wheel.

I hopped out and went into the restaurant—I'd learned to trust his instincts. "*Buon giorno, buon giorno*," I called out into the silence. A young man appeared and I asked if dinner was being served that evening.

"Yes, yes, but it is a meal of only fish."

"Great, fish," I assured him, wondering why he was warning me about fish, the Mediterranean was directly in front of me. I watched over his shoulder as he wrote our reservation in his book. *Due stranieri*, we were the two foreigners, no names required.

> Like an orchestra warming up, each couple began to add sounds to the room. "Hmm." "Ohh." "Ahh."

We never found the church that afternoon but at 7:30, pressed and dressed, we returned to the restaurant. The entrance was dark, but the little dining room glowed. Six tables were dressed in crisp white linen and lit from above by globes of hand-blown glass. The young man who had taken my reservation introduced himself as the chef's son. "Come in, come in. *Prego, prego*."

A local couple dressed for a special occasion joined us; a German couple who'd hiked up from the train station completed our party. The dining room sat suspended at the edge of the cliff. Our table had a prime view of the curve of the bay and the rugged outline of the peninsula that hid this spot from an army of tourists nearby. A few lights sparkled in the town below as the sun faded and we turned our attention to dinner.

Edoardo, playing host and sommelier, poured champagne and set out a bowl of pine nuts and white raisins. Polite greetings passed among the three tables and then we began to eat. Our first course was a delicate octopus and tomato salad. Local white wine replaced the champagne, Edoardo attending to each of us as if we were his only guests. Like an orchestra warming up, each couple began to add sounds to the room. "Hmm." "Ohh." "Ahh."

Sautéed squid glazed in an earthy porcini mushroom sauce followed—it slid down silky and smooth. Then came calamari and vegetable tempura, light, fluffy as lace, and topped with crunchy black caviar. We six guests were starting to nod at one another in appreciative accord. We savored each dish and luxuriated in each wine. The grand maestro in the kitchen, as yet unseen, had us in his control. The portions were perfect and I sensed that he was determined to take each of us all the way to the end of the meal.

He slowed our pace with an intermezzo of aioli whitefish and then a clatter from the kitchen announced the end of our pause. Edoardo emerged with inky squid stew. As soon as each table was served, as soon as we were caught in the rapture of the ink, he popped out of the kitchen with his camera and said, "Cheese." We were caught with black teeth and dirty napkins. By now the six of us were laughing and talking the international language of food. Even the older Italian couple, serious about eating and a little reserved, was laughing along with us. The Germans, world travelers, second-time diners here, were eating at full tempo. The noise in the room had peaked and we were having a party.

Without announcement maestro Compiano made his appearance. In chef's hat and apron, a Santa with cherry-red cheeks and a smile, he came in carrying his masterpiece: six baby lobsters, steamed bright orange and sporting tomato-red pinchers, climbed the sides of an upright celery stalk. We gasped. Then one tiny lobster at a time, we deliriously ate our way through to the finale. Symbols crashing, violins playing madly, I could hardly hear from the sounds of pleasure in my head. Our eating was done, our ohs and ahs subsided, and our conversations returned to our individual tables. Only then I remembered Edoardo's warning about fish—fish, fish, only fish—and I smiled.

The chef returned with his crepe cart for an encore. From a pan of flaming banana liqueur, crepes were the closing cadence, our sweet goodnight kiss.

Last to leave the party, Jeff went to settle our bill and I went to gather our coats. When Jeff did not return, I knew he had made his way into the chef's kitchen. I heard the sound of two cooks talking the common language of food, and I put our coats back on the hook. The night was about to begin anew—just as it had after meals with gangsters in Rome and farmers in Umbria. This time we would be sharing the ritual glass of *grappa* with Signore Compiano.

Late afternoon light woke me the next day and I finally asked, "How did you know last night would be go great?"

"If a place can survive for so long that far from the waterfront, it must be good," he said. Simple. Instinct.

That night in Liguria, Jeff and I had slid from our parallel universes into a new one together—and we didn't want to go home.

⌒

Bonnie Smetts is a San Francisco Bay Area art director and writer who spends part of each year in Italy. She is currently consumed with conquering Romanaccio, the notorious Roman dialect, and sharing her rocky road to fluency as a guest columnist on italian.about.com. Her story "Turquoise Dreams" appeared in The Best Women's Travel Writing 2006.

4

AIMÉE DOWL

MAMMONE MIO

Or, how to understand Italian men.

MY LOVE OF ITALIAN CULTURE CAME RELUCTANTLY. I GREW up in a noisy and argumentative Italian family, enjoyed innumerable Christmas lasagnas, and despite the avoidance of my heritage, I somehow ended up becoming an Italian teacher. Having been reared in a plus or minus fourth-generation Italian family in which the mother tongue had been lost decades ago, I didn't learn *la bella lingua* at home. Instead I studied the language in hometown Italian classes. Fortunately, with the help of language, my predictable adolescent disdain for the *familia* evolved into a full-fledged love affair with the country of my ancestors.

My Italophilia continued to grow as I made short trips to the Mediterranean. From post-pubescence to the present, I have been exploiting every possibility to fund my excursions. First, it was the parents, then it was junior year abroad, then it was waiting tables, but my friends insisted that what I needed was an Italian *ragazzo* to host me. While my passion for the *bel paese* has always been expressed in consumption of espresso, gelato, art, literature, fine leather, and fashion, it has rarely been expressed as a passion for Italian men. In fact, crystalline memories of my male relatives has somehow turned me off to that half of the Italian population, despite the real capability of one Tuscan boyfriend to get me a visa.

When I experienced a temporary crisis of loneliness in my mid-twenties, it only seemed logical to my lady friends that I find a nice Italian guy on one of my summer expeditions. I shrugged. I'm an independent woman who hardly needs a man to make things happen. And anyway, my mental images veered toward the negative end of the Italian male stereotype: macho, homebound, and self-absorbed. Loneliness is a powerful motivator, though, and loneliness in one of the world's most romantic destinations is even more motivating. After all, I should adore Italian men! I'm an Italophile! Perhaps I had been unfair to millions of eligible men for comparing them to my uncles and cousins? Maybe I was denying my philia to a majority of the Italo?

Not only was I committed from that point to being more open-minded about Italian men, I was also going to make a concerted effort during my summer in Italy to get to know them better. I was on a manhunt.

When I arrived in my northern Italian summer digs, located about halfway between Venice and Trieste on the tiny island of Grado, I ran the risk of getting to know more about German tourists than Italian males. But I immediately initiated my research by talking to every local guy in sight: the bus driver (large, gregarious, eager to invite me aboard his vehicle), the landlady's son (lithe, soft-spoken, and constantly banging at the pipes), a fisherman on the quay (rugged, strong, and odoriferous). My concerted open-mindedness was yielding fruit. A diverse spectrum of Italiani were imprinting my newly receptive brain. Even if I wasn't about to cure my loneliness with any of them, I was discovering a desirable strain of habits and attitudes among men who were available and remotely in my age range. These kindnesses included a chivalric propensity to opening doors, a dazzling mode of dress and orderly grooming, and a swarthiness capable of inducing mild perspiration. Nonetheless, memories of my Uncle Lou devouring *mostaccioli* rekindled my fear and stalled my chase.

In the middle of June, I headed over to Milan and asked my friend, Rafaella, who happens to be a psychologist, about these recurring and disruptive memories of Italian men and Italian food from my childhood. Walking around the interior of the Milan cathedral with her elbow hooked around mine, Raffa immediately put things into perspective: "*Sai*...food and men are preoccupations for every woman. For Italian women, it is even more the case. The recurring images of your uncle and homemade pasta are a signal to embrace these things, not reject them."

"Yes," I replied, "you and your mother have a wonderful closeness, but do you ever do your own laundry?"

Moving my eyes from one saintly statue to the next on the towering cathedral walls, I thought this was an odd place to be talking about *inciting* lust. I also thought that it might be a sign. Apart from her divinely sanctioned psychoanalysis, Raffa cleverly lured me into another therapeutic experience: we went to an InterMilan soccer game. Seeing Baggio's strong silhouette running across the field pushed Uncle Lou's image out of my mind once and for all. Thanks to Raffa, I was ready to embrace the Italian male.

As I embarked, Raffa reminded me of a couple of important things before undertaking my safari. Embracing the Italian male means embracing his family, too. An increasing percentage of Italian men between eighteen and thirty-four years of age are living at home—nearly 60 percent by 2001. This means that close to two-thirds of eligible single men in Italy are living with their parents.

This reminder prevented me from gasping when I met Giuseppe while admiring a statue of the Grado's patron, Saint Eufemia, and learned that he lived under his mother's roof. Giuseppe was an incredibly stylish and intelligent man. His being stylish was not shocking as many Italians are inherently so; a traveler in Antarctica once noted that even in the polar nether regions Italians out-styled the other nations' research teams with their modish parkas and excellent food. Standing before Eufemia on a hot June day, with slightly perceptible breezes winding their way from the Adriatic into the piazza, I imagined Giuseppe looking quite handsome in handcrafted Italian snow gear. Yes, Giuseppe was *di moda*, but he was also smart and funny. It was not long before I was introduced to his equally modish, smart, and funny siblings, all of whom lived in the home of his mother and late father.

In fact, I soon found his family's company invaluable: one evening I learned many new tidbits about Giuseppe as I was strolling through the ancient town square with his sister, including that he had been unemployed for quite some time. Giuseppe had characterized it as "underemployed," mixed with continued graduate studies during the academic year. I suddenly felt a nauseatingly familiar feeling of being duped into going out with a loser, but I swallowed a glacier of *stracciatella* off my mountainous cone of gelato and tempered the information with my knowledge of the country's socioeconomic situation. Italy is a place where the young, energetic, intelligent, and educated are often left searching for a job, and it is also a place where many adult children live at home because of this dearth of opportunities. Tight family units, conservative social values, and clingy mothers also account for the phenomenon. The Italians even have a word for fellows who stay close to home: *mammoni*.

So do Americans: mamma's boys. In Italy, however, *mammismo* is a fact of life for adult children, while in the U.S., where housing is more ample and unemployment is lower, being a mamma's boy suggests a kind of wimpy, puerile dependence.

One of the reasons that many American women experience culture shock when they date Italian men is precisely this lack of privacy that comes from dating a *mammone*. While I have done no scientific surveys on cross-cultural relationships, I have known many American women who are at first enamored with the tight-knit intimacy of their Italian partner's family, only to give over to a profound resentment of their companion's mother and the constant comparison of her own inferior cooking to that prepared by the household's matriarch. My stateside friends have either bailed out of their relationships with *mammoni* or gotten married to bail their *mammoni* out of relationships with their mammas.

Despite my *mammone's* sister's insistence that her brother was a great guy and my own confidence in his charisma, I was feeling the fear grow like Dante's trepidation as he entered the ninth circle of hell. Walking arm-in-arm with Giuseppe's sister, my personal Virgil, across the piazza, I turned to ask her: "What's ahead if he doesn't get a job?"

She assured me by saying, "Oh, don't worry, he can live at home as long as he wants!"

Knowing this was true, I tried to embrace the reality, pushed memories of Uncle Lou out of my mind, and decided to have a little fun with the *mammismo* that was rocking my independent American worldview.

A number of years ago, the television newsmagazine, *60 Minutes*, aired a segment on the *mammoni* of Italia. Apparently, the whole country has seen it because almost every Italian male responds to it by dismissing it. Italian men do not reject that the single portion of their sex are living at home in large numbers and that many who don't live at home anymore are still sending their laundry back to their mothers on a weekly basis, but they do reject that they rely on their mammas for everything and that their mammas are reluctant to give them up to an independent life. In fact, the very mention of *60 Minutes* can incite a virulent denial of *mammismo*. When I casually brought the show up over espresso, standing at a café near the sea, Giuseppe choked on his sip, pursed his lips, and simultaneously waiving his hand and shaking his head, clarified the idiocy of the program's points about all these mamma's boys.

"What is wrong with living at home? In the United States, the family is so fractured. Here, we have to live at home, and we are very close."

He was right, at least about his own family, and also about mine. But I had also seen how "close" Giuseppe's mamma was with his laundry and the dishes and all the domestic work in his large household.

"Yes," I replied, "you and your mother have a wonderful closeness, but do you ever do your own laundry?"

"Of course!"

"Really?"

"Well, sometimes."

"How often?"

"I don't know."

"And do you cook...ever?"

"Yes, I cook all the time"

"Pouring cereal at breakfast doesn't count!"

"I don't eat cereal. Cereal is disgusting. Mamma makes... uh..."

"A-ha, I knew it! I bet you've never cooked in your life!"

Giuseppe threw his hands into the air and insisted that charging him of *mammismo* was unfair because his mother absolutely loved to cook and clean for him, and if she couldn't do it, she would be depressed and lost. Wanting to rest my case, I suggested that he try cooking and cleaning for himself for a week, as a test. He agreed, but it took no more than two days for me to realize the futility of his effort and the perseverance of his mother in supplying him with superb homemade food and crisply starched shirts. I also remembered that I, who hadn't ironed a shirt since my last job interview, didn't hold a candle to Giuseppe's mamma when it came to cooking and housekeeping.

In order to further my research and to enjoy the growing affection between Giuseppe and me, I proposed a weekend away from family and all discussion of mothers. I planned an excursion to Venice. It was late July and the city was teeming with summer energy and throngs of foreign visitors. We steered cleared of Saint Mark's square and explored the outer islands. With my escort, who knew Venezia like a doge's gondolier, we explored the labyrinthine canals and passages for the best gelato, pasta, and wine. After three days of eating up the city and not a word about the banned topic, Giuseppe brought up his mother.

"You know," he said, "I would like to live away from home, but I can't. There is no point in me setting up a house on Grado because I don't want to live there in the future, and how can I afford an apartment in Venice or Milan? It's impossible, you know. At home, I have everything I need, and I am not a baby. I can come and go when I please."

"Yes, I know," I replied in an apologetic tone, "I am sorry if I implied that you are a baby, and I am sorry that it is so hard to find work."

When we returned to Grado, I was more comfortable with

the realities of *mammismo*, if not still occasionally skittish about dating a *mammone*. Giuseppe and I were having a genuinely thrilling time together, and he was helping to dissolve my misgivings about Italian guys. I even began to really appreciate being around Giuseppe's family, taking special notice of how courteous he was to his mother and appreciative he was of her cooking and cleaning. He said "*Grazie*" and "*Te amo, Mamma*" often, and he reciprocated by helping out with tougher household projects that she was too frail to do herself. Among Italian men, I had often been afraid of *machismo*, but instead I got *mammismo*. And I thought I could live with that.

Late July bled into August as I lost track of the days. I spent an enormous amount of time with Giuseppe—and his family—and I was excited about all the new Italian language and culture I was imbibing. Grado's tourist season kicked into high gear, and the little island was flooded with Germans who flee to Italian beaches every August. My days with Giuseppe were limited, and my loneliness began to return as I realized that I would soon have to leave my *mammone* and head home to my single life. I was delighted, however, that my manhunt had successfully enriched my appreciation of Italian men, opened my mind, and eradicated my fears and stereotypes. I really had roped a nice guy, and I liked him for a lot more than his ability to get me a visa.

My imminent departure was on Giuseppe's mind, too. Having seen most of the cultural offerings of the area—the ancient architecture of nearby ruins, the top of every climbable bell tower within a day's drive, the artistic treasures of Trieste and Venezia—we had taken to walking along the sea in the cool air of the early evenings. Within days of my departure, however, we could no longer avoid the topic of our approaching separation.

"Will you return to Grado next year?" he gently asked.

"I don't know."

"You should. You have many friends here. My mother adores you," and after a pause, he added, "and so do I."

I told him that I was sad to have to go home and that he had made the summer wonderful. I had not said anything during the entire season about my initial hesitancy to date an Italian, but I dared to tell him then.

"Thanks," I concluded, "for showing me how wrong I was about Italian men."

"See," he said, "we are not all helpless *mammoni*." And after a moment of silence, he suddenly turned rather serious, looked out over the glistening water, and then turned back to me, "You might even find that you would like to spend your life with a *mammone*."

It was a profound statement for which I was totally unprepared, and I hid my childish anxiety by looking down to the cobblestones. My philia for the Italiano seemed palpable, strange, and real. I stood in my own awkwardness, praying inwardly for the right response. After a seemingly endless silence, Giuseppe's *telefonino* rang. Thankful for the interruption, I tried to stir myself from my stupor. Just as I was coming out of it, I heard Giuseppe say in a frustrated but responsive tone, "I'll be home soon. *Ciao!*"

"Who was that?" I asked.

And despite my appreciation for the disruption of Giuseppe's cellular, I realized exactly who had rung him up, and it reignited my consciousness. It was Mamma, and she wanted to know when my *mammone* would be home for dinner.

Aimée Dowl is a freelance writer and teacher who winters in the Andes, and when she saves enough money, summers in the Apennines.

5

JASON WILSON

PIEVE SAN GIACOMO

An American student is embraced by an Italian family and a heartfelt gift.

ON MORNINGS LIKE THIS, WHEN YOU WEAR MY MUSTY old bathrobe, I can feel the terry cloth weight of responsibility. I can smell obligation in those damp sleeves. I can see simple truths revealed in the way it hangs slightly opened, untied, as you blow-dry your golden hair.

Make no mistake, the robe is ugly. Heavy and not quite soft, it's cut too big, the unnatural material too unabsorbent for drying completely after a shower. The pocket sits too high for any hand to rest comfortably inside. A mixed floral pattern, muted goldenrod and dirty white, extends from the collar to the knees. From a distance the color is reminiscent of used manila envelopes. Yet you continue to grab for the robe behind the bathroom door as you shiver on cold days and it often appears burdensome as it drapes over your smooth skin.

But there is another thing. These mornings, when I

see you in that robe, I also am reminded how lucky I am to have not one, but several families including one in a dusty little village in Italy's Po Valley. There, on a hot July day, I lounged in my pretend aunt's whitewashed courtyard with my pretend mother while the sun reflected off tins of biscotti and bottles of sparkling water. The two women watched, giggling in Cremonese dialect, as I ate meats, breads, and pastries they'd carefully prepared and drank the Coca-Cola bought special for me in the city.

And on these mornings, when you smile at me in the mirror as you brush your teeth, I'm once again nineteen years old, studying abroad for the first time. Once again I am sitting in that Italian courtyard, not quite mature enough to grasp the complex familial duties I'm expected to carry out. Once again, for just a moment, I live in Pieve San Giacomo.

"The Bernabé family specifically asked for the boy," Professor Causa said with a wink when she greeted me at the elaborate arched doorway of the Circolo Fodri, our school in the small city of Cremona. Inside, a dozen men and women attired in designer suits and silk dresses smoked and drank coffee and nibbled treats. They filled the hot, muggy air with Italian language in a way I'd never heard before, certainly not the laborious "*amo, ami, ama*" I was accustomed to hearing in the black headphones of the college language lab back at the University of Vermont. I was lost as I shook hands and uttered a meek *piacere* when presented to a man wearing Gucci sunglasses standing next to his bleached-blonde wife.

I heard my professor repeat to Sara and Jen, two of my fellow students, that "the Bernabé family specifically asked for the boy." I scanned the room and realized I was the only male out of seven students. And since I was also the youngest—just a sophomore—I assumed that also made me the only boy. All around the room, fellow students were paired up with the well-dressed couples smoking cigarettes.

Then, as if they simply materialized from the swirl of language and heat and smoke and silk and laughter, the Bernabé family was thrust before me. A round, red-faced bald man with a giant mole on his thick neck waddled over, dressed in neatly-pressed polyester pants and a short-sleeved dress shirt. The man reached for his gray-haired wife's arm, tugging instead at her stiff blue housedress. The two of them beamed as they approached, while behind them trailed one of the stylishly dressed young women with long brown hair. Professor Causa introduced the family: Paolo, Anna, and their twenty-seven-year-old daughter, Daniela. Paolo slapped my shoulder and put his arm around me. Anna kissed my cheeks. Daniela took my hand.

From then, I can only remember the stern warning from my professor: "Daniela works in the local tourist office," she said. "She speaks perfect English, but I've explicitly told her that she's not to help you at all unless there's a real emergency. You are to have total immersion."

I was whisked away in a dark blue Fiat and we rode through the busy streets of Cremona into the countryside. I sat in the back with Daniela, and Paolo kept looking at me in the rear-view mirror with a big grin on his face. Anna asked me dozens of questions, little of which I truly understood. When I turned to Daniela for help in translation, she smirked and shrugged her shoulders.

At great speeds, we passed yellow and green fields, patches of blood-red flowers, and farmhouses with terra cotta roofs. Fifteen minutes outside of Cremona, I began to worry about where the Bernabé family was taking me: all of the other students were staying with families only a few blocks from the Circolo Fodri. Anna started speaking louder and slower, as if I was retarded or deaf. I was dripping with sweat, but I couldn't think of how to ask Paolo to roll down the windows.

Soon, I saw a little blue sign for Pieve San Giacomo and Anna turned, tapped my hand, and shouted, "We are here!" The Fiat pulled into the gates of a dusty yard, past farm equipment. We parked beside a lush vegetable garden, more red flowers, and a patio with a fountain. Puppies and kittens roamed freely.

Paolo grabbed my bags, escorting me through the red drape hanging over the door and onto the cool stone floor of the house. Anna led me into my room, showing me my towels, my drawers in an ancient oak wardrobe, my orderly bed. Outside my window, chickens strutted in the yard next to a doghouse.

That night, at dinner, Paolo passed around a plate of prosciutto he'd cut on the meat slicer in the kitchen. He uncorked an unmarked bottle of red wine. The television news on RAI UNO droned as white noise in the background. Anna disappeared and reappeared from the kitchen with plates of melon, spinach, pasta, *fagiuolo*, veal, bowls of the sharp Grana Padano cheese of the region. By my third glass of wine, I was beginning to understand more and more of what everyone was saying. Every time a dish was served, Paolo slowly explained where it came from. "All of this meat, it comes from my cows. The vegetables, from my garden. The grain, from my field. And the wine, it comes from my grapes." In fact, the only thing in the kitchen that looked storebought was the Coca-Cola Anna had offered me when we walked in the door.

Between the pasta and the main course, I carried my dish into the kitchen. Anna quickly shooed me away saying, "No, no, no, no," and dragged me by my arm back to the table, laughing.

Later, as we drank coffee and Paolo poured cognac onto the fresh kiwi gelato, Anna turned to Daniela and asked, "Americans eat breakfast, right?"

My ears perked up. It was the first phrase spoken at normal speed which I completely understood. I was elated.

"*Sì!*" I said, nearly jumping across the table. "We eat breakfast every morning at home." *Colazione. Colazione.* Breakfast. Oddly enough, it is still perhaps the most beautiful Italian word I know. Anna smiled. Her wide blue eyes flashed at Daniela with a look of pride. She spread her arms. "Big?"

"*Sì,*" I replied.

"Tell me," she said. "What do you eat for breakfast?"

That's when I was stuck. Visions of pancakes, waffles, muffins, Pop Tarts, and Cap'n Crunch floated through my head. But I had no dictionary nearby and I didn't know any of those words. Everyone at the table watched patiently as I stammered. Then suddenly, I remembered a vocabulary list from the previous semester. "*Uova!*" I shouted.

"*Uova?*" Anna said. "Very good. There will be eggs tomorrow morning at seven o'clock." Things had been settled. After coffee, we all went to bed.

The next morning, the following headline appeared in a local newspaper: "Vermont college students are Cremona's guests."

During our first days at Circolo Fodri, I asked Professor Causa, "Why do they say things like *Cuma veet* instead of *Come vai*?"

She chuckled. We were on our morning coffee break and English was allowed. "I assumed that might happen," she replied. "Signor and Signora Bernabé speak in dialect. It's probably been a long time since they studied the Italian you're learning. In many ways they are meeting you in the middle when it comes to language."

"It's difficult to follow."

"Maybe they will teach you their dialect, as well." Professor Causa finished her cappuccino. "Back to class," she said. "*Allora, parliamo italiano.*"

That first week, we reviewed nouns and present tense verbs. We wrote out dictation quizzes. I tried to do my homework the best I could after drinking many glasses of wine at dinner each night and then grappa in my coffee.

The reading from the first chapter of our textbook, *Vivere all'italiana: A Cultural Reader,* was due on Friday and I translated it at lunchtime on a park bench near Cremona's cathedral while Sara and Jen and Lisa drank aperitifs at the café near school. The translated essay was entitled "*La Famiglia Italiana*":

> Italy, therefore, presents the character of a society in transition, divided between the old and the new, between tradition and modernity. The family reflects this contradiction and strains to compromise. Many parents today are more open to dialogue with their children and inclined toward self-criticism. The majority of young people maintain affectionate relations with their parents, and in general the profound sense of devotion and responsibility between them remains unchanged.

"*Su! Su!* Jason!" shouted Anna at 7:12 A.M. "*Tardi! Tardi!*" The light switch for my room was situated in the hall. Anna flicked the light on and off to wake me even though I'd only overslept a few minutes.

When I sat at the table, two fried eggs were waiting for me— just as they were each day for twelve weeks. Paolo returned from the morning inspection of his fields and read the newspaper, RAI UNO still droning on the television. Paolo poured a shot of grappa into his coffee cup. Meanwhile, Anna raced back and forth, urging me to eat faster or I'd miss my train.

This was the routine, established from day one when I inadvertently left myself an extra forty-five minutes to catch the thirteen-minute train from Pieve San Giacomo to Cremona. After that, no matter how late I stayed up the night before, my bedroom light flicked on and off sometime around seven o'clock. Every day, I arrived in the city much too early for class.

On that first day of school, Anna gave me a green child's book bag, complete with a colorful tag on the flap for my name and address. Daniela left for work in Milan later than usual so she could escort me into Cremona. I tailed along like a little brother, book bag on shoulder, as Daniela showed me how to purchase tickets. Then she showed me to a compartment where she introduced her friends, Mariangela and Christina, both stunning with long, curly black hair, dressed in chic Milan outfits, and wearing sunglasses.

When we arrived in Cremona, the four of us walked to Daniela's favorite coffee bar and ate brioches with other fashionable people, me in shorts, sandals, and a "Free South Africa" t-shirt. The women introduced me to the barista as "Jason, our American friend" and everybody laughed when he yelled, "Ah, Friday the thirteenth!" and ducked behind the bar. After coffee, Daniela slipped me a few lire to make sure I had enough money for lunch and instructed me on which afternoon train to ride.

Each morning after that, in Daniela's absence, Mariangela and Christina doted on me as they went to work at the hair salon and the shoe store. The two of them didn't speak English, but wanted me to tell them all about New York and its nightclubs and they laughed and flirted and invited me out to discos at night, even though they knew Paolo and Anna would never have allowed it.

I usually returned home to Pieve San Giacomo alone on the train. Paolo was often in the garden, with tall rubber boots glistening in the bright sun, picking asparagus or spinach for dinner. Inside, a Coke was poured and waiting. Anna ironed in the living room or worked on the sewing machine or stood in the kitchen shaping tortellini with her finger. My laundry sat neatly folded on the bed. Once, I had located the washer, but was chased away by Anna, who squealed and said, "Men don't know how to use this."

On those hot afternoons, young men, Bernabé cousins, stopped over on motorbikes and scooters to discuss *Rambo* and Schwarzenegger and auto racing. Shy little neighborhood girls came to the patio so they could play with the puppies. They blushed and giggled when I poked my head outside. The television was tuned every afternoon to World Cup games, which Italy hosted that summer, or to an Italian version of *The Price Is Right* called *O.K.!*

One day, I met Daniela after school and she took me to meet her boyfriend, Massimo, who lived in Cremona near a violin-making school which Stradivari had attended. Massimo was a painter who shared a studio with several other artists and Daniela was obviously smitten with him.

We hung around all afternoon, as Massimo, in paint-splattered clothes, wild hair, and a goatee, sketched and paid little attention to me. Meanwhile another young artist painted a watercolor of me on brown paper.

When we arrived home after dusk, dinner was ready. Bowls of minestrone were served and I mentioned to Anna that I'd met Massimo. She smirked and glanced at Paolo. "Do you like him?" she asked. "His long hair?"

"Sure," I said.

"He's an artist, you know." Her smile grew and she raised her hand to shoulder level. "With long hair."

Anna poked me in the side and chuckled while Daniela blushed and tried to sink into her chair. I smiled, now reveling in the role of annoying little brother. Daniela was thoroughly mortified.

"Oh, Massimo is nice enough," Anna said.

Paolo grunted. "He's crazy," he said with a wave of his arm. "Just crazy."

At that, Daniela sat straight up and loudly began defending her Massimo. Paolo winked at me and shook his head. "Crazy!"

Late that night, Daniela brewed coffee and the two of us stayed up and, for the first time, really discussed anything in English. "You seem tired," Daniela said.

We talked about Jack Kerouac, whom she had just read. Then we joked about the "De La Soul" t-shirt she wore and how she hadn't realized the phrase was the name of an American rap group.

When my train stopped in Pieve San Giacomo each afternoon, I often traveled the remaining mile alone. Sometimes, I heard the children who rode their bikes nearby tell each other in loud whispers, "That's the American," and I waved. But most often, the walk was a chance to clear my head from a full day of lecturing and to prepare for a full night of conversation.

My classmates could stay at the cafés in Cremona until late, drinking and complaining about what a taskmaster our professor had become. Each afternoon after class, we sat and watched German tourists come in and out of the cathedral and spoke English in purposeful slang so no one could understand us. I generally was compelled to leave after only one or two bottles of Danish beer.

And so I would return to my family. In the fiery sunlight of the late afternoon, I followed the road home between fields and grain towers. Golden brown dust levitated in the hot air. On some particularly tough days at class I would walk the road cursing my situation, angry that the Bernabés frowned upon me staying in town to hang out with my friends. Instead, I had to phone my friends and plan to be dropped off and picked up or arrange a sleepover as though I were thirteen. If I took a different afternoon train home, even if it was six minutes later, I made sure to call.

The road to the Bernabés' eventually brought me past a white iron gate and the home of Daniela's aunt. Once she'd learned my daily schedule, Aunt Gina would be waiting for me in the yard. "Jason! Jason! Come here! It's your *zia*," she said, her jet black hair pulled straight back, her eyebrows meticulously plucked, and her makeup unmarred by the heat. She gripped at the white bars of the gate and asked me if I liked the flowers in her yard. Every day, Auntie begged me to come in for a snack and I always evaded her by politely declining, saying Paolo and Anna were awaiting me at home.

But soon, Aunt Gina appeared at the gate with treats. A bottled water or a Coke in the afternoon. Then, she began waiting in the mornings as well. She dangled bags of cookies through the gate. "Share them at school," she said. And, always, she implored: "Please, some day, come by. I'll make you lunch or dinner or just a snack."

After about a week of this, I asked Paolo and Anna about Aunt Gina. They smiled sadly and shook their head. "*Che peccato*," Anna said. Paolo told me she'd lost her husband the year before.

One morning, when I stepped outside on my way to school, Paolo was sitting on the patio smoking a cigarette. He stood and waved for me to follow him. We walked along the edge of the farmyard and then toward a shed. "In here," he said, motioning at the door. I walked through the shed door and immediately faced a slaughtered cow carcass hanging on the wall, blood dripping on the floor. A half-dozen women from the village, including Anna, sat at a long table slicing slimy pieces of red meat and dividing the good stuff amongst themselves. My stomach wretched in the stale air.

Paolo said something in dialect while all the women looked at me and giggled. He then put his arm around my shoulder and explained that this was one of his cows. I was too shaken to really listen to his explanation, but it was obvious Paolo was proud that one cow could provide food for so many families.

When we returned outside, Paolo lit another cigarette and returned to the patio, quite pleased with himself for giving me such a shock so early in the morning. "The men, we only slaughter the cow," he chuckled. "It's the women who have to do the rest." This was not the first time the men of Pieve San Giacomo tested me.

Earlier in the week, two of the Bernabé cousins—young Paolo and Mirco—stopped by on their motorbikes and asked me to play soccer. Since I'd already bragged about playing the sport since age five, and since no one believed me, I was forced to prove myself. We rode through tiny streets to the dried-out fields where a dozen teenage boys kicked a ball around. Mirco introduced me as an exchange student and one of the older boys asked, "What is he, German?"

"No," Mirco replied. "American."

"American? What does he know about *calcio*?"

We played six a side and, right from the first touch, everyone on my team passed the ball to me. Meanwhile, everyone on the opposing team rushed to defend me. It must have been because I was at least three years older than the other kids, but I easily dribbled through the defenders. I drew the goalie out of the net and rocketed a shot past him that hit the upper corner of the net.

"Are you sure he is not German?" asked the older boy.

I scored several more times that afternoon and the boys invited me to play in their big weekend match. I returned home for dinner with dirty knees and grass stains on my shorts.

Paolo returned from the local café not long after I did. He entered the dining room and said, "The word in town is that the American is very skilled, a great player." He smiled. "You could play in the first division." This was exaggerating quite a bit. But still, the words he used—*un bravo giocatore*—filled me with the kind of pride only a father can bestow on a son.

It is six years later and my family—my real American family—is seated in a restaurant. I have just finished translating the words "rabbit" and "apple" from the Italian menu and now my real mother understands what's in the risotto special.

"It's a shame you don't practice your Italian more often," she says. My real father and real brother rip off hunks of bread and dip them in oil.

"When is the last time you contacted Paolo and Anna?" my mother asks.

"Two years ago," I reply. "During the World Cup when Italy was in the finals."

"That's a shame," she says. "They were both so good to you."

An uncomfortable silence hangs over the white tablecloth. My mother smiles and pretends as if this is just small talk. Just normal dinner chit-chat.

My father tries to fill the silence. "Didn't you tell me Paolo had his leg amputated a while ago?" he says.

"Yeah," I mumble with a mouth full of bread.

"Well, I hope you go back there some day soon," my mother says with a sigh. "You'll regret it if something happens to one of them."

I chew my food knowing that I've had opportunities to return to Pieve San Giocomo but have chosen to travel elsewhere for many reasons. My family has moved on to another conversation but I am far away, wallowing in regret. I am reminded of the night I decided to stay in Cremona and drink in bars with my friends. I believed I'd clearly explained my intentions that afternoon over the phone to Anna. That I'd miss dinner, but not to worry, I'd eat a pizza in town. Sara, an Italian friend Pietro, and I drank bottle after bottle of wine beginning directly after school. When I finally decided to go home, dusk had been hours ago. Daniela and Paolo were waiting for me at the train station, headlights on in the pitch black. Both frowned. "Did you have a nice adventure?" snapped Paolo.

"I'm sorry," I said. Daniela remained silent.

At home, Anna was standing in the doorway, her face flushed with fear. Inside, dinner was sitting on the table, cold. I sat down to eat it. I tried to say that I'd explained myself over the phone, that we'd had a communication breakdown. But my Italian failed me. All I could do was repeat, "I'm sorry, I'm sorry," over and over. I went to bed. The next day, two eggs sat on the table, Anna flashed her smiling eyes, and Paolo returned from the bakery with a brioche. And nothing more was ever mentioned of the incident.

There were no other photographs of sons or daughters, only Jesus Christ hanging over the sofa.

Salad is served in the restaurant and I've yet to say a word since we ordered. My mother tries to bring my head back to the table. "Don't worry," she says. "They know you'll come back to visit."

But what about the robe? you ask. *What does the robe have to do with all this?*

Everything, I tell you.

On a hot Saturday in her courtyard, I was finally ensnared by Aunt Gina. On that day, Anna and I rode bicycles—Paolo was off in the fields and Daniela joined us after working in Milan. We arrived at Aunt Gina's house to find a great feast prepared. Aunt Gina pulled me into the yard by my arm and I wasn't allowed to leave my seat until I had gorged myself on every dish set in front of me. Sweat trickled from my every pore while the women carried trays back and forth.

Then, when I could eat no more, Aunt Gina insisted I tour her house. The three of us entered the cool, dark living room, lighted solely by strips of sunlight through nearly drawn drapes.

Aunt Gina fingered a yellowed photograph of a young man in a soldier's uniform, and told me it was her husband. There were no other photographs of sons or daughters, only Jesus Christ hanging over the sofa.

Aunt Gina motioned for me to stay where I was and shuffled down a long hallway. "*Che peccato*," Anna whispered and crossed herself. We waited for what seemed like twenty minutes and could hear her rummaging through the bedroom, calling, "*Un momento, un momento!*" Finally, she emerged from the hallway gently carrying the robe.

She thrust it into my hands and urged me to slide it on over my clothes. I complied, wrapping it around my Grateful Dead t-shirt and tying the sash tight around my waist. Silence enveloped the dark room. I stood with my arms wide, modeling the same robe her dead husband had worn each morning while he sipped his coffee and read *La Gazzetta dello Sport*.

"*Che bello!*" she exclaimed. Then she burst into tears and hugged Anna, whose eyes also welled up.

"You'll promise to wear this?" she asked.

I stood dumbfounded, staring at the sleeves of the huge, ugly robe, not believing this whole presentation could be for me. Me. The one with the already stuffed backpack. The one preparing to shove off in two days for the rest of Europe. I knew I had no choice but to make room. To smash down what clothes I could and inevitably leave some of my other things behind. I had no choice but to carry the heavy robe.

And I have. I've carried it through more than ten moves, from dorms, to apartments, to houses. I've carried it in trunks, in trash bags, in a box shipped by my real American mother, a woman who has always understood the value of things like robes and small feasts in widows' courtyards.

Now, years after the semester abroad, Aunt Gina is dead.

Paolo walks with a prosthetic leg and doesn't leave the house much. Daniela still lives at home, and she and Massimo are still only friends. I hear from Anna infrequently, but from what I can read, she still makes sure the Bernabé house runs smoothly. The few letters I send are written in English for Daniela to translate; any Italian proficiency I once possessed is certainly long gone.

Yet each morning, at our home so far away from Pieve San Giacomo, you reach for that robe behind our bathroom door. I chuckle to think this is what you wear before dressing in your fashionable skirts and pants. At times, the robe makes me hungry for fried eggs—a food we never eat because, of course, eggs are much too high in cholesterol and because we have promised each other to try to stay healthy.

Other times, I can't help but ask if there is something else you'd rather wrap around your body. "I don't want a new robe," you say, so simply and beautifully. You giggle, amused to watch me fumble while learning my new role as husband. Right then, I know I am hopelessly entangled by my families—all of them—including the one the two of us are just beginning.

Jason Wilson is the series editor for Houghten Mifflin's "Best American Travel Writing" series.

THE PARTISAN ARTISANS OF THE OLTRARNO

Behind Florence's tourist façade lie serious creative endeavors.

"WE LIMIT TOURS TO THE FLORENCE ARTISAN SHOPS, BE-CAUSE they don't like too many customers," said Rosy, my bilingual guide.

"The shop owners don't like customers?" I asked.

"No, then they'd be too busy. Too many demands. That's why they don't have signs on their shops. They only want the sort of customer who already knows who they are and what they do, and can afford to pay for the best."

"Well I don't know a thing, and can hardly afford the gelato here. Will I get past the front door?"

"Don't worry, I'm taking you in the back."

I had asked Rosy to give me a behind-the-scenes look at the workshops of the famed artisans of Florence.

I wanted to find out about the people as well as their crafts. Rosy was a working artisan herself, an apprentice gilder, so could offer me a true insider's view.

Many of Florence's craftsmen are the fifth generation of their family to ply the same trade of woodcarving, shoemaking, paper-making, or metal work. Often they use techniques and materials unchanged since the Renaissance. Some artisans claim direct lineage to a relative said to have carved frames for da Vinci, to have inlaid the marble floors of the Medici Palace, or bound the first edition of Galileo's teachings.

Rosy and I began our walk to the Oltrarno district of Florence, literally "the other side" of the Arno which divides the city. The Oltrarno is much quieter and less touristed than the Statue-of-David, special-price-leather-jacket-for-you main part of Florence north of the river. We left the tourist-filled thoroughfare to enter winding streets so narrow the three-wheeled "Bee" mini-trucks nearly scraped the stone walls as they made their buzzing deliveries of the artisans' raw materials of wood, marble, dyes, and metals.

"After forty years of working in this shop, I have done almost everything it is possible for a man to do with metal."

Our first stop was at a set of nondescript double doors with thick, knotted wood and dirty windows, the same look as any other on the side street. No store name, operating hours, or even a display case marked this as a shop. We entered to an extraordinary clutter of tools and twisted metal objects, all hanging from tables, walls, and the ceiling. Flickering fluorescent lights illuminated stained and gouged metal and wood workbenches. It looked like a high school shop class where two dozen students had just dropped everything and bolted for lunch. But all this was the work of one man. When he saw me enter his workshop area, owner Giancarlo Giacchetti extended his large clenched fist in my direction. I recoiled, but he wiggled it around as an offering until I realized I was supposed to shake it. He didn't want to stain me with the grease covering the palm of his hand.

As Rosy explained my interest in his craft, Giancarlo walked past sets of huge ornamental gates, the railing of a staircase, and a series of elaborate bed frames before stopping proudly before a giant fish. His thick, dirty hands darted back and forth like large blackbirds while he explained the process of crafting the giant aquatic creature.

Rosy translated. "After forty years of working in this shop, I have done almost everything it is possible for a man to do with metal. Now, I am retired, on a pension, but what else can I do with my free time? Metalwork is my passion. And the fish, they are the passion of my passion." He outlined how he treated the metal by melting wax on top of the piece, and dipping it into a silver bath, allowing the statue to oxidize to create the shimmering aquatic colors in his school of bronze fish.

"Oh sure, I do the big money jobs, the typical stuff, the gates, the bed frames, it helps to pay the bills. I was just in San Francisco, doing a wrought iron staircase in a downtown mansion. The family, very famous, they even knew Sharon Stone. I met her, but *fffft*," he flicked his hand dismissively, "too skinny."

"I also went to Cleveland, spent six months there," he continued, "A rough town, full of Sicilians. No, I think I like Florence the best. It is a traditional city of artists, and better yet, a city of artisans."

I asked Rosy about the difference between an artist and an artisan. She smiled. "There's something special about getting your hands dirty, building calluses while working the tools and the wood. A craft just seems more real, more solid, than painting. I guess that's why I got into gilding picture frames. It grounds you, makes you feel like you've created something tangible. You can always debate if something is art or not, but a good frame is a good frame."

Perhaps in this search of something tangible, Oscar-winning actor Daniel Day Lewis dropped out of Hollywood in 1999 to spend a year as a cobbler's apprentice in the Oltrarno. To this day Lewis refuses to talk about the experience, preferring to keep this spiritual retreat to himself. The cobbler felt fine with chatting to a reporter, though. He complimented Lewis's hard work but noted Lewis was a little high-strung, so to speak, when a shoe wouldn't turn out just right, saying, "I used to tell him, 'Daniel, no one is perfect.'" But the shoes must be close to perfect to merit the $1,500 sale price per pair. Or perhaps it is their unique imperfections which create their value.

Rosy took me down another side street to the shop of Giuliano Ricchi, an artisan whose skill was to eliminate imperfections in his metallic jewelry box templates. Word of his talent and creativity has spread worldwide, as buyers from Neiman Marcus and Christian Dior purchase many of his designs. Giuliano led us through a small archway down into the sub-basement of his shop to see his "factory." A single iron stamping machine stood on a table in the middle of a narrow room with shelves filled with design templates. His machine looked like a relic from the nineteenth-century industrial revolution, with its thick iron form, its crashing cranking sounds, and the dangerous stamping motion with which it imprinted a template onto a copper covering.

Upstairs, in a pleasant showroom facing a garden, Giuliano pointed out one small jeweled pillbox on display. "Bill Clinton bought one when he was here," he said as an aside. I wondered if it was for Monica. It seemed perfectly appropriate, and even expected that in a half-hidden jewelry shop in the Oltrarno, in the shady south side of the river, that a man would be shopping for his mistress.

Like many artisans, Giuliano's business was a one-man show. When he was out to lunch, or on vacation, the shop was shut. And without children to follow in his footsteps when he retired, his business would end. While his metal templates would remain, the knowledge of a lifetime of creative effort would be lost. His outmoded equipment would be scrapped, his narrow building probably turned into a refurbished guest house for visiting art hounds.

But for some, the craft continues for another generation. At a papermaking and bookbinding shop, we stopped to watch another artisan in action. Enrico Giannini, the proprietor, with his pointed beard and mischievous smile had the air of a vaudeville magician. And he welcomed us with an almost magical demonstration of his craft of mixing ink for paper designs. He dramatically yanked a kerchief covering a pan of water, and turned off the fans. He pulled a porcupine quill from a quiver of tools, then used his other hand to drip inks onto the surface of the water. He used the quill and a giant comblike device to pull through the ink clouds, creating a series of swirling patterns. He then overlaid a sheet of paper on the surface, which soaked up the ink to create a unique marbled design.

Enrico's ingredients had an element of witchcraft, incorporating a red from the crushed bodies of an African beetle, and the water infused with extract of Irish seaweed. He bound one of his books with the skin of a stingray, the shape of the pointed tail embedded in the cover. His shop had many custom pieces and antique restorations, but plenty of smaller gifts as well, a nod to the increasing number of tourists finding his shop.

Enrico showed us an old Tuscan cookbook on a counter, midway in the process of restoration. His thirteen-year-old grandson was working on rebinding it as a birthday gift for his grandmother. The old magician beamed. "Soon," he said in accented English, "the family will have another artisan."

As we left the neighborhood Rosy pointed out a marble memorial plaque created by a son for his artisan father. The grey words were carved on the wall above the closed door of an antique restoration shop where an angry lion statue stood guard. In severe angular lettering the carved words declared the creed of the Oltrarno. "Here Giuseppe Maioli, maestro and artisan, lived, worked and suffered for his art."

Bill Fink lived, worked, and suffered writing the Florence, Tuscany, and Umbria sections of the guidebook Pauline Frommer's Italy 2006. *His writing has also been included in the Travelers' Tales anthologies:* The Best Travel Writing 2006 *and* What Color Is Your Jockstrap?

DAVID YEADON

THE SYNERGISM OF LITTLE KINDNESSES

It could happen to you!

BE GENEROUS—IT'S THE NATURAL THING TO DO, AND IT comes back in equal measure.

It was approaching Christmastide in Italy's Abruzzi Mountains, which could explain this series of small but significant events. Or maybe not. Actually I believe they could happen anytime—all it takes is that first little spontaneous act of kindness to set the whole synergistic, cause-and-effect magic into almost endless, rippling motion.

I was stuck. My camper had broken down in a forest in these wild Apennine ranges that swirl and buckle their tortuous way down the length of the country, virtually to its very toe at Reggio di Calabria. After a bit of pathetic fiddling and banging and cursing (I'm not much of a mechanic), I decided I was likely to be here until morning. I'd seen very little in the way of traffic, discounting something resembling a wolf that, at dusk, slipped boldly out of the forest and stood watching me for an unnerving length of time, and two well-lubricated youths on those ghastly mopeds that firecracker around every nook and cranny of this otherwise delightful country.

But I was wrong. Someone was coming in a car. The driver stopped at my insistent waving and got out, all smiles and seasonally happy, took one look at my "foreign" engine, and said he'd take me to the next village, about ten miles down the road.

He dropped me off at the only gas station in the place and refused any offer on my part of a thank-you gift—money, a cigar, a bar of chocolate, which were all I had with me. He explained my predicament to the mechanic, a middle-aged woman. In no time the woman and I were beetling back up into the forest in her tow truck. She seemed amused by me or by my appearance or something. And then I understood. "You—San' Claus," she giggled. "Big!" She rubbed her stomach. "Ver' white!" She pointed to my beard. I nodded and smiled. This had happened before on my journeys but not until, for some odd reason, my once Irish-auburn beard had suddenly turned completely white a couple of years back despite the fact that my head hair remained exactly as ever—a kind of bog-country brown.

And cakes. Gorgeous cream and chocolate delights just begging to be eaten on the spot.

We arrived at the camper. Nimble as a chipmunk she was out with her bag of tricks and literally, within three minutes, had the creature purring contentedly again with none of the banging and cursing and expletives-deleted that had accompanied my useless efforts.

Again I offered payment. She refused and giggled once more

at my appearance. "Just like San' Claus!" before scrambling back into her truck and suggesting I follow her back into the village.

Well, that was one problem solved. Next was food—a bakery for some bread for dinner. And cakes. Gorgeous cream and chocolate delights just begging to be eaten on the spot. I congratulated the baker on his fantastic array of chockablock-calorie cannoli and he was apparently so pleased at my compliments and my efforts at Italian 101 vernacular that he presented me with an extra little hazelnut and caramel vanilla-cream puff-pastry creation in its own little box. His wife stood by nodding and grinning. I thanked him profusely and moved on to the next store, a pharmacy, to buy some supplies for a cold I felt coming on. Again, as soon as I walked in, the Santa Claus routine started up and the two older women behind the counter put on little girl faces and asked, "Where are our presents?!" So I played along, wondering what I could give them that might have a little of the seasonal spirit in it. And of course—what better than the boxed masterpiece of confectionery presented to me by the baker and his wife?

"Have you been very, very good?" I asked in my deepest Santa voice. "Oh yes, yes! Ver', ver' good," they responded in delighted Italglish as I gave them the cake and left the store buoyed on waves of giggles and gasps of delight. Suddenly a hand was at my elbow. One of the women was tugging me back inside and the other one, coyly and shyly, came around the counter with something behind her back. "For you," she said and handed me a large box of chocolates all adorned in Christmas motifs. I tried to refuse but they'd have none of it. "No, no—you take—eat.." and they nudged me back into the street, still giggling, "San' Claus need," and they patted their stomachs like kids.

A box of Italian chocolates! What a lovely surprise. I opened them up and twenty beautifully decorated bonbons stared expectantly up at me. What a splendid addition to my dinner. Except... no, they weren't really mine. I had people to thank. So back I went to the bakery and showed them the chocolates and asked them to help themselves. They were delighted and carefully chose one each. "No, no!" I said. "Please take more." And after much encouragement I persuaded them to take six—and then there was one more for an old man coming into the store for his evening loaf. He almost lost his balance, he was so surprised.

And then the mechanic lady. I went to the end of main street and there she was, busy with someone else's car. "Aha!" she grinned. "San' Claus!"

"Yes," I said. "And here's a little gift specially for you," and I made her take half a dozen chocolates.

So that left seven chocolates. Still too many for me. I asked if she knew the man who had given me the lift into town in the first place. She nodded but was not sure where he lived.

So I went out onto the street again, chocolate box rampant and in real Santa Claus mode (I was beginning to enjoy this role now). I handed out one chocolate each to any stranger who had the semblance of a smile. Which was just about everyone I met, so my seven chocolates rapidly diminished to one. "Mine!" I thought, and salivated.

And then, who should I see coming down the village main street with his dog but the man who first helped me back in the forest. I pushed the box at him, tried to apologize for only having a single chocolate to offer, and almost bludgeoned him into accepting it.

And that, I thought, was that.

But no. I was wrong. The man, who fortunately could speak a little more English than most of the villagers, invited me to accompany him for a drink at his local trattoria which, of course,

I willingly accepted, and this, believe it or not, led me to one of the best weeks I've ever had in Italy. For, it turned out, this man was the bocci champion of the village (apparently a position of considerable prestige) and he decided San' Claus needed a place to rest to enjoy the abundance of the season. Which I did and which is a whole other tale. Suffice to say, for a few days, the village took me in and made me part of itself, sharing its festive joy, its food and drink, and its heart—many, many hearts—and all because of that man's one tiny act of spontaneous kindness way back in the forest.

⌒⊃

A native of Yorkshire, England, David Yeadon has worked as an author, illustrator, journalist, and photographer for more than twenty-five years. He is the author of numerous books including, A Season in Basilicata, Seasons on Harris, *and* The Way of the Wanderer, *from which this piece was excerpted. He is also a regular travel correspondent for* National Geographic, National Geographic Traveler, The Washington Post, *and* The New York Times. *In between travels he lives with his wife, Anne, in Japan, where she is a Professor in Vision Rehabilitation, and also in a Hudson Valley lakeside house, just far enough north of Manhattan to preserve soul and sanity.*

8

A COLD DAY IN THE DOLOMITES

LAURA READ

Italy in the spring? Forget it—go in the winter.

"Kabow!" A cannon shot thundered over Italy's Val di Fassa, jolting the pack of cross-country skiers around me into a double-poling frenzy. Meanwhile, I stood in the start tracks, frozen.

After slapping my thighs and stomping circulation into my limbs for two post-dawn hours waiting for the race to begin, I'd succumbed to a Dolomite deep freeze.

This was serious. I was starting one of the longest cross-country ski races on the planet, the Marcialonga, which covers 70 kilometers of hilly terrain through two of Italy's most dramatic valleys. Twelve sets of parallel tracks guided skiers out of the start zone, where they double-poled in order to avoid breaking each others' slender skis and poles. After one-quarter mile, the tracks merged into a wide skating trail, which had been machine-groomed to velvet the night before.

Having never done this race, I was relegated to the

eighth starting wave. I had watched my husband, Doug, and 3,500 other skiers, zoom off ahead of me. Low morning sun sent cool beams across the ice-blue meadows. Now it was my turn, and I couldn't move.

Whack. The guy behind me prodded my calf with his pole and hissed.

Stabbing my poles into the brittle snow, I folded forward at the hips, cracked through my frozen muscles, and used all my back and ab power to *push*! Skis slithered forward. *Push*! Lats swelled with strength. *Push*! Legs shifted into the side-to-side skating glide.

Historically, I hadn't been the competitive type. In high school, I'd skipped swim practices for afternoon movies. Later, I'd found boyfriends in coffee shops instead of on ball fields. Then I had met Doug. In the blush of new love, he'd taught me how to skate-ski. Soon enough, I was hooked on glide. Now, struck by a coldness I'd rarely felt, that hook had thinned.

"Go, girl," I whispered. "You've been chomping for this all year." True, I'd been leaping diagonally up hills, roller-skiing into the dark, balancing on wobbly plastic discs—all for...what? To feel like Otzi the Iceman, the 5,300-year-old mummy vaulted down-valley in a Bolzano museum? My goal had been to finish in fine form, and happy. Right now I just wanted to go to bed. One consolation: I wasn't alone. Problem was, most of my peers were well ahead.

The Marcialonga is the second longest race in a world series of cross-country ski marathons organized by the Worldloppet Ski Federation. (*Loppet* means "citizens' race" in Swedish.) The series bundles fourteen of the toughest masters events in Europe, America, Asia, and Australia. Up to 80,000 distance junkies compete every year. The longest course is Sweden's 90K Vasaloppet; the shortest, the 42K Engadine Marathon in Switzerland. With its intimidating length and daunting name, the Marcialonga is a favorite among distance-crazed skiers. I was performing among the sport's elite—and way out of my league.

Racers also love the event for its beauty. The course makes a boomerang U through two Dolomite valleys, the gentler Val di Fiemme and the higher, more geologically dramatic Val di Fassa. From the start, in the village of Moena, the route climbs 300 meters over 20 kilometers. At the U-turn, in the town of Canazei, it crosses the Avisio River, and returns down-valley for 50 kilometers. Near the finish, it climbs a 300-meter hill in a heart-bursting 4 kilometers to end in Cavalese, where Doug and I had rented a room in a farmhouse inn.

By the time the first of the route's many gentle slopes lay behind me, my fingers were stiff as cannelloni. If my breath could shatter into crystals, it would. The "happy" aspect of my goal was ebbing. Then a small miracle occurred. I rounded a hillside to see a tremendous, shimmering set of monster peaks, their gold and silver façades flashing in the sunlight. Soaring high above the spiky pine groves, they seemed surreally alive. If they could speak, they'd urge me on—or laugh. Estimated to be some 240 million years old, the peaks tell geology's greatest stories of heat, violence, and the passages of time, of oceans abandoning spines of coral reefs, fires rifting the earth's skin, and new formations rising in the grinding and folding pressures of moving tectonic plates. At dawn the mountains resembled Hogwarts villains. At dusk, they glowed like butterscotch.

Adventurers look to the mountains for inspiration or chances to prove their strengths and skills. Closing my eyes, I wished for each of these. I tasted butterscotch.

When the trail plunged to the snow-packed streets of Soraga, it split into strands in order to get us safely through the old hamlet's narrow passageways. I squeezed through an alley not fit for a mule, then grunted out of town and up the next hill. Steeple bells clanged.

Although my brain heated up with mental effort, my limbs stayed cold. The towns of Vigo di Fassa, Pozza di Fassa, and others blurred by, the sun rose higher, but the air temperature sank. That's when a nasty thought snuck in for an ambush. "You could hop a bus and go eat strudel."

I shook a pole. "Out, fiend!" My skis skittered on ice.

In the next village, a crowd gathered, hoods frosted white. Through the cheers, an unfamiliar voice called: *"Brava Laura! Bravissima!"* A woman waved a Marcialonga event guide at me. Of course! She had located my bib number and name, and shot an arc of encouragement across the sharp air. I hooted back, "Yee-haw!"

At 20 kilometers, Canazei hosted the first rest stop. The town is the tourist gateway to the imposing Sella Group, a golden fortress of sheer-sided rock. Mountain-lovers visit from all over the world to hike, climb, ski, and bicycle among its thirteen peaks.

A warm sport drink tasting like orange chalk sloshed heavily on my tongue. Someone brushed my elbow. Just then, an Italian, frosty curls rimming his hat, said, "Is that you, Mrs. Read? How are you doing?" An incredible coincidence! Last week, I'd met him skiing on groomed tracks in a valley to the north.

His lusty accent bloomed images of linguini, fettuccini, and ravioli in my mind. Rubber lips muffed my words. "I'm not sure I can finish—too dang, freezing cold."

"But it is all downhill from here. And the sun is warming up the day. You can certainly make it, Mrs. Read."

"Call me Lauowwrrda." The Italian version of my name sounded earthy. It was stacked with fortitude, like the name of someone with Val-di-Fassa thighs and a Sella-sized ambition, someone who could power through the Marcialonga, lickety-split. As Lauowwrrda, I could finish the race—maybe even in fine form.

The man motioned to leave. "We will help each other."

I crammed two cookies into my cheeks and off we went, across the bridge over the Avisio River and down the other side of the valley. There were still 50 kilometers to go.

On the Marcialonga web site, the cartooned race map had represented the course as a piece of licorice winding among a dozen snow cones. At home, I'd assumed the cones were cute exaggerations of hills. A few kilometers after Canazei, when skiers bunched to a congested stop before a white wall, I learned they weren't.

Instead of stamping and groaning—as I wanted to—however, people were giggling. Some big-armed guys made jokes. Skiers who'd scouted the course earlier in the week explained in broken English that the downhill on the other side ended in a breakneck curve. As I huffed my way up, two Norwegians called "Hup, hup, hup!"

On top, someone warned the downslope was a mess of snaky ruts. Imagining myself a linguini doll, I absorbed the bumps with the flexibility of fresh-cooked pasta, cresting the snakes, zipping the corner, and—*swoosh*—entering a village where hundreds of fans screamed "*Brava! Brava!*" Happiness flooded my chest. I was skiing in good form.

The track spun me out of town and into, suddenly, silence. Sunlight lit fiery crystals in the snow. The track widened next to a flat section of river. This was perfect for the V2! Best for flat terrain, the V2 technique produces long, joy-filled glides punctuated with balanced, rhythmic, side-to-side poling.

The end was near—maybe 20 kilometers away—and so was food! Between the aromas of wet river bank and musty willow, I could almost taste the things I yearned to eat: strudel, lasagna, locally made sausages and cheese, and a kind of dumpling special to the region called *canederli*, often made with speck, liver, cheese, or sometimes spinach or mushrooms. Dolomite cuisine reflects a definitive mix of Italian and Austrian cultures. At different times, Etruscans, Romans, and Franks ruled the region. From the 1400s until World War I, Austria and Italy split the reign. Today, food, handcrafts, architecture, place names, personalities, and languages resonate the enduring blend.

A gurgle sounded behind me, and I thought it was the river. Instead, it was my Italian friend. Snow splattered his Lycra pants from a fall. I beckoned him to ski beside me—the trail was wide enough—but he declined. "No. I learn from you." Many people ski for years before mastering the V2. I used my simplest words to explain the technique, and then we flew.

I may not own the fast-twitch muscles of sprinters, but I have my own winning tool: a second wind that during many a long training session had powered me home. However, at the Marcialonga's last food stop, my second wind had expired. Volunteers were serving espresso in thumb-sized cups. I chugged three, and skated into the final challenge.

The trail, warm now and slushed out by thousands of skis, disappeared straight uphill into a forest of spruce once harvested for Stradivarius violins. I put my head down and started up.

Another miracle occurred. Caffeine buzzed my veins; my body felt light as a sunbeam. A third wind had arrived! In a whirl of last-ditch strength, and deliriously chanting "Marcia-longa" to Mozart's "Don Giovanni," I streamed past a dozen tired skiers. At the top, although front-runners had finished hours ago, fans still cheered from the bleachers. Above the din, a race-rough voice I knew very well soared, "Laura! Laura!" High in the stands, brighter than the rest in his red fleece, Doug was testing the bleachers with wild jumps. That's all I glimpsed before crossing the painted line and folding in half.

I had finished! I'd skied 70 kilometers in five hours, fifty-two minutes. As the late sun turned the mountains into heaps of massive butterscotch strudel, my day ended with double portions of polenta, sausage, and mushrooms, and, finally, the flannel sheets of a farmhouse bed.

From the subarctic tundra to the mountains of South Asia, Laura Read explores connections among self, community, and the environment with pen in hand and lens to the world. Read's stories and photos have appeared in the San Francisco Chronicle Magazine, *the* San Jose Mercury News, Sunset, Walking, Nevada *magazines and others. She is a contributing editor at the* Tahoe Quarterly *and creative director at Juniper Creek Publishing.*

9

MICHAEL SHAPIRO

UNDER THE TUSCAN SKY

An afternoon with Frances Mayes in Cortona.

TO MY UTTER SURPRISE, FRANCES MAYES MET ME AT THE train station. I had disembarked in Camucia, about three miles from the hilltop town of Cortona, where Mayes lives with her husband Ed in the now legendary Bramasole, the house she made famous in her millions-selling book, *Under the Tuscan Sun*. Fortunately I recognized Mayes from her book jacket photos. I approached her and asked, "Are you Frances?" and she broke into a broad smile, saying she figured it'd be nicer if they picked me up so I wouldn't have to take a cab to Cortona. It was a gesture that embodied the southern hospitality of Mayes's Georgia roots and the generosity of spirit of rural Italy.

I had come to Cortona to interview Mayes for my book *A Sense of Place*, a collection of interviews with the world's leading travel writers conducted at their homes. After flying into Milan and visiting with old friends in Venice,

I took the train down to Florence and on to Camucia, the station closest to Cortona. It was a mild December day, just weeks after the film *Under the Tuscan Sun* premiered on thousands of screens in North America. From the station, Ed drove up switchbacks in an assertively Italian style while Frances noted the historical sites: "That's where Hannibal defeated the Romans in 217," she said, pointing to the valley nestled into the time-smoothed hills below.

In Cortona, Frances showed me the Teatro Signorelli, the grand historic theater of archways and green shutters that made such a strong impression in the *Tuscan Sun* movie. Walking along the village's narrow streets, she stopped to chat with a florist, and then we had a simple yet richly satisfying pasta lunch. To complete the meal, the osteria's owner brought us each a chilled glass of sea-green *alloro* (bay laurel liqueur), a gesture emblematic of the Italian warmth and kindness that Mayes, an accomplished poet, so eloquently evokes in her books.

So
they always saw
this big empty house on
the hill and some
people thought it was haunted.
A lot of people used to climb
up and take the wild lilies
and daffodils and irises,
the cherries.

Under a dark gray sky, we drove past a massive Etruscan wall, whose boulders date back to 800 B.C. "We have workers today," Ed said as we pulled into Bramasole's driveway. "As usual," Frances replied. Located just outside of Cortona, Bramasole is an imposing three-story house, approached by a slate path flanked by roses, sage, and rosemary. You could call the color of the house peach or terra cotta, depending on the quality of the light hitting it. Part of the exterior has peeled away to reveal the stones beneath.

The land, a plot that would take two oxen two days to plow as stated in the property's ancient deed, is dotted with olive trees.

Alongside the house is the Strada della Memoria, a thoroughfare lined by 600 cypress trees, each a tribute to a soldier who died in the first world war. Mayes had won a $10,000 award from Barilla, an Italian pasta company, and donated the money to Cortona to replace dying trees and to install plaques with the name of each soldier.

Before we sat down for our interview, Frances gave me a tour of Bramasole—I was especially moved by the muted blue and orange pastels of the fresco she and Ed discovered while refurbishing the house. After our hour-long chat, Frances showed me the sturdy "Polonia" stone wall on the way out and stopped for a moment so we could quietly admire an arched shrine built into another wall nearby.

What follows are excerpts from our conversation revealing the essence of Bramasole, Cortona, and small-town Italian culture.

What first attracted you to Italy and what kept you coming back?

I studied Renaissance art and architecture in college, so I especially wanted to come to Italy to see the things that I had studied. But of course the minute I got here, I saw all the Italians in the piazza greeting each other and having coffee and enjoying life. I said to my husband then: "These people are having a lot more fun than we are—what's going on here?" What keeps us coming here forever is the people—that was the beginning.

This house is called Bramasole, which you say means "yearning for the sun." Beyond the literal meaning, can you tell me what that symbolizes for you?

When I came here and got out of the car the first time, a real estate agent said, "*Bramare*, to yearn for and *sole*, sun, something that yearns for the sun." That just really hit, because metaphorically I was hoping for a connection with the light, something transformative, something big. So the name of it immediately made me think, I would like to live in that house because that house is already very much at home in the landscape. It's been here; it's going to be here; anything with me is just going to be a passing through. The house itself is very important on this position, and if I can live in the house I think I can learn from the house how to live here in Italy. And that has been the case actually—it's been the house that has led us here, that profound sense that there's the Etruscan wall, the Medici wall, this house, the valley down below where Hannibal defeated the Romans. It's these literal layers of history that you fold yourself into, and if you feel at home there, something radical has changed in your mind. It changes you.

You write in Under the Tuscan Sun *that you and Ed were not going to have children but that this house would be your child.*

I'd have to revise that statement. It's been more that we have been the children of the house because it has taken the lead and introduced us to the culture. This house was abandoned for so many years, and it's on this Strada della Memoria, this street out of Cortona where all the local people take their walks—they're passing here every day. So they always saw this big empty house on the hill and some people thought it was haunted. A lot of people used to climb up and take the wild lilies and daffodils and irises, the cherries. They had used the land as they were growing up, so they had a relationship to the place. They were particularly intrigued by the crazy Americans who had taken on the project. And they did think we were nuts because nobody in Cortona had ever bought this house. Now they say to me, I could have bought that house.

In the beginning it was working on the house, actually doing the work that gave us a place in the culture. I think working on the house probably saved us five years of getting to know people. Because we were working along with a lot of Italians here, they saw that we were actually on our knees cleaning the bricks, and on the ladders cleaning the beams. We weren't just standing there with our hands folded, giving directions, but we were in it. And I think that made them feel that they could invite us, and they began to very quickly bring us gifts: eggs, olive oil, bags of spinach, things from their own land. Then they began to invite us to their christenings and weddings—it was through the house that we were able to get to know people and to be recognized in town.

There is a wonderful kind of gift exchange among people who know each other here. Yesterday, Beppe brought us eggs, Giorgio brings a bag of wild boar, Giuseppina brings biscotti. We take people things from our garden—there's this kind of constant giving. You find things left on your doorstep, squashes and melons, you don't even know who left them.

What have the most exciting discoveries been?

The way of life here, the gentleness and the great good manners people have, the hospitality, the generosity, those things have just been huge gifts. We love the people here, they're fun. They do their work, but they're not work-obsessed. They always have time to stop in, to go have a coffee. We had a coffee with the police chief this morning. It's more intimate here—it's partly that it's a very small town, but there's more to it than that. There's a sense of delight in living here. People love their town, they love their history. The Tuscans are nasty and fatalistic and cynical, too— they're not simple, happy-go-lucky, welcome everybody, that's it. They have a lot of levels, and they're very critical: they will tell you what they think of your garden or your clothes. They're very blunt in a way, but they're complex. There's this underlying basic generosity and sweetness that you can revel in here.

We like the life in the piazza, the constant interchanges that you have with all kinds of people, all kinds of classes, all kinds of educational levels. There's not as much stratification as we felt in our lives in America, where college teachers hang out with college teachers and writers with writers. Here it's not like that, it's everybody and you find yourself having dinner with all kinds of people—it's fun. It's interesting too because you get such a variety of perspectives and personalities and histories.

I wonder if your books have helped Italians more greatly appreciate what it means to own a historic house in Tuscany. I know they appreciate their heritage and their history, but do you think that you as an outsider could look at this house with fresh eyes and say, this is a treasure. Whereas people who have lived here thirty years might say, it's just an old, abandoned house.

Definitely. That's been kind of fun. When I first wrote *Under the Tuscan Sun*, my friend, the writer Ann Cornelisen, said the Italians are not going to like it. And I thought, Maybe not, it's such an American perspective. But much to everybody's surprise, they did like it. It was a bestseller here. I've had hundreds of letters from Italians saying, I never appreciated my own country until I saw it through a foreigner's eyes. And I'm so ashamed that it took a foreigner to show me (laughs). It made them happy and proud.

When I wrote *Under the Tuscan Sun*, I changed some people's names for their privacy. I never thought anybody here would read it because I never thought it would be translated into Italian.

After the book became popular in Italy, people from town came up to me over and over and said, "Signora, why did you change my name?" They wanted to be known. And now it's really quite moving for me that often very old people in town come up to me and say, "I want to tell you something because you can write about it." That impulse to have your life mean something, to go beyond your own memory, is very surprising to me and I've heard a lot of wonderful stories. I've actually written some of the things that people have told me about: walking back from Russia after World War II, just stories. To be known as the town writer, even in such a small town is nice.

One question about food and dining here in Italy: what do you find so appealing about the food, the dining, the sharing, and all that you write about?

The food reflects the culture so much. Food always reflects culture, but here it's even more than in other places because there is still the sense of the long table, the table that's endlessly accommodating. The fact that someone shows up for dinner with two friends that you haven't invited used to shock me, but the assumption is, there's plenty, and it's fine to bring cousin so-and-so. At home if somebody brings the children and you haven't invited them, you think, Oh my Lord. But here it seems fine.

The philosophy of the long table reflects the kind of relationships Italians have with their family, friends and neighbors. The grandmother's at the table. There is not an exclusion of people—there's an inclusion. Yet the social life here is absolutely crippling. I get exhausted here from the social life—you're invited constantly. You could go out every single night of the week, and it gets exhausting. The food is always fabulous, but sometimes I think, Please, I just want to stay home one night.

But they think that eating alone is sad. And they think it's unhealthy. When Ed's here by himself, he never, ever, gets to eat at home alone. Our neighbors, they love him, they say, "You come to our house, you're not eating alone." And that's just the way it is. Even in restaurants, like today, after we had that very simple meal, there's the little gift of the laurel liqueur that they make and give to their friends when they come in. It's always something more than just what you pay for. There's always the gift. The sense that, we're having polenta tonight, come on over. The sense that we're out walking and we find some wild asparagus, come to my house, let's make a frittata. You eat together, you eat, it's ancient and basic.

Now it's early December and we're coming into winter. This is a time when far fewer travelers visit, but it seems to be a very nice time to be in Italy. Could you say a word about the low season and about the change of seasons here?

I love staying here in the winter because it is so quiet and the food is different every season of the year. If you're here in the winter, all the hunters are bringing in their woodcock and pheasant, and wild boar, and wild mushrooms, and chestnuts. A whole different thing appears on your plate in the winter than in the spring and summer and fall. Florence is much more wonderful in the winter when all the tourists clear out. It returns to itself. You see the Florentines in their woolens having hot chocolate and you just get more of the sense of Florence as a place where people actually live.

I like the change of seasons here. We do have changes of seasons in California, but they're subtle. Here they're very dramatic. The spring is just astonishing. The whole place is covered with wildflowers and the little wild asparagus are coming up, and the green almonds that you eat raw, all the little fava beans and wonderful little lettuces are coming up. So every season has its own culinary pleasures, and I like that very much.

The changes in the food are also the changes in the activities. You go looking for mushrooms with friends; you go into the woods and pick up chestnuts. In the early spring you start looking for the asparagus. In the summer, it's the little wild strawberries. In the late summer it's the blackberries. People do all these things together so the table again is not just the eating, it's the whole way that food becomes part of your life and part of the table. You are bringing things to the table that you've grown and found. It's a profound difference from going up to Whole Foods.

There's no place like Italy because Italy has it all: the beauty of the landscape, the people, the art, fantastic cuisine and wine. Everything for me comes together here. Sometimes people say to me, "Your books are popular because Italy is so trendy; next year it'll be Morocco." And I think: No it won't, because they say Rome is the eternal city, Italy's just got that eternal aspect to it. It can't be duplicated. France has a lot but it doesn't have the Italian people.

I remember that image near the end of Under the Tuscan Sun *of you as a four-year-old girl jumping out the window of your home and running. I wonder if all this, this house, this life, is ultimately fate or will, or some combination of the two?*

Probably a combination of both, but that little moment of climbing out the window is kind of the impulse: Go. And I always feel that, I feel very split always between the desire to stay, the desire for home, the desire for the nest, the desire to gather people around in the home, and that equal passion to shut the door and go, to leave it all behind and seek what's out there. So I think for me the writing partly comes from the tension between those two things. And it's odd because they both involve a sense of place, the place being the home, the domestic, and then the place being out there to be discovered.

Michael Shapiro is the author of A Sense of Place: Great Travel Writers Talk About Their Craft, Lives, and Inspiration. *For two years Michael interviewed the world's top travel writers where they live: Jan Morris in Wales, Tim Cahill in Montana, and Peter Matthiessen at the far end of Long Island. Among the other writers he interviewed for* A Sense of Place: *Bill Bryson, Pico Iyer, Isabel Allende, Simon Winchester, and Paul Theroux. Shapiro's essay about completing this project while his father was suffering from inoperable cancer*

appears in The Best Travel Writing 2005. *Michael lives with his wife and cat in western Sonoma County, about an hour north of San Francisco. He volunteers as a guide for ETC, a group that takes disabled people on sea kayak and river rafting adventures. To read excerpts from that essay and from* A Sense of Place, *see Shapiro's site: www.nettravel.com.*

10

THELMA LOUISE STILES

STANDING IN LINE

What does it mean in Italy?

ONE WINTER MORNING IN PORDENONE, A SMALL BUT BUSTLING city in Friuli-Venezia Giulia, Italy's northeastern region, I enter the offices of the telephone company for the first time and take my place at the end of a line. Ahead of me are three customers. Several minutes pass. Then I notice something peculiar. The third person in my line has a counterpart to his right. The second person in line also has a counterpart to his right, as does the first person in line. There appears to be a formal queue—mine, I am reasonably certain—and, to the right, an informal, perhaps symbiotic queue.

Slightly troubled, I begin taking stock. The parallel queue to the right isn't far enough away from *my* queue to be a separate, distinct line, I reason. Furthermore, I see only one official behind the counter and that official is helping the people in *my* line. Observing these details, I come to the conclusion that the people in the parallel line are relatives or friends of the clients standing in *my* line. I relax.

A fifth person arrives and falls into line behind me. Seconds pass. Then I notice something strange: the man behind me seems to be slowly moving forward. Suddenly, he appears at my right shoulder. *What's going on?* I wonder. *What in the world does he want?* Well, nothing, apparently, for the man standing next to me never acknowledges my presence, never utters a single word. Despite feeling uneasy, I try to ignore him. But after several more minutes pass I begin to grow impatient. I would like to put this intruder in his place. B*ehind* me.

Unless you nail his shoe to the floor, an Italian shopper standing in a queue is likely to stray.

By now, I am visibly agitated. Yet my twin seems comfortable exactly where he is. When I finally arrive at the counter and begin my usual florid hand gestures and garbled Italian, he is still at my side. His elbow rests on the counter. Hunched over, he hovers a mere half-inch away from me. I can smell his cologne, hear his rhythmic, raspy breathing. I suspect that he's enjoying the show, that he's smiling sardonically or perhaps even wincing in pain as I try to wrap my lazy lips around his beautiful, mellifluous language.

Here in Livorno, a seaport town in the Tuscany region, a variation of the same phenomenon occurs often. Time after time, while I'm standing at the end of the line in the Coop, the supermarket where I purchase groceries, I am asked: *"Lei é l'ultima?" Are you the last?* I used to wonder why a shopper, seeing me, clearly standing at the end of the line, would ask, *"Lei é l'ultima?"* or *"Chi é l'ultima?"* But now I get it. The question is necessary because here in Italy the last person to arrive in the line could be anywhere.

In front of you, for example. Or perhaps in the Coop's coffee bar, enjoying an espresso.

Unless you nail his shoe to the floor, an Italian shopper standing in a queue is likely to stray. You see, conventional lines are unimportant here. In the States, vertical lines, for the most part, remain vertical. In Italy, queues quickly disintegrate. Some years ago, I rushed into the lobby of La Gran Guardia in Livorno, the birthplace of opera composer Pietro Mascagni, to buy a ticket for a concert commemorating the fiftieth anniversary of his death. I was trying to hurry. So were others. I wanted a ticket for one of the cheapest seats in the house and was fearful the theater had sold out. At first I was waiting with about five other people. We had a nice, fairly neat little line going.

Then pandemonium: scores of patrons, also late, also seeking tickets, rushed into the lobby. I recall feeling a growing sense of panic. *What was happening to our line?* I craved a well-defined, vertical line. An orderly sequence. I was uncomfortable with the horizontal line that was forming, fearing no one would remember who came when, or who was next. People who had piled in several minutes after my arrival were hovering to my left and my right. Finally, I could endure no more. Throwing up my hands in exasperation, I cried out in English, "Look, who's next?" Silence. The people surrounding me must have thought my outburst a bit odd. I certainly did.

At the Puccini festival held each summer in an outdoor theater at Torre del Lago Puccini, a beautiful lakeside area near Viareggio, a similar mishap occurred. During the intermission for "Madame Butterfly," my friend Giuliana asked me to wait in front of one of several outdoor coffee bars along the perimeter of the theater while she rushed over to find out whether her daughter and grandson and our buddy Miranda wanted some espresso or gelato for refreshments.

In seconds, I was surrounded by a group of heat-besotted opera fans, all of them determined to get something to eat or drink before the start of the final act. Miranda and Giuliana had to rescue me. As I was wobbly-legged and dizzy, they guided me away from the throng of patrons and over to the metal stairway leading up to the area where our seats were located. I sat on a cold, dusty step. I rested my head between my knees.

To queue or not is a heated issue for those of us who live in Italy but grew up in the United States or Great Britain. We view the Italian tendency to break formation as a character flaw. It's not that Italians get in line and then leave, asking if you would mind watching their space while they dash over to aisle 5 to pick up a bottle of capers. That would be understandable. And it's not merely that they spot a friend standing in an adjacent queue and insist on straddling both lines so that they can gab a little. No. Something more significant is going on.

I've spent more than a little time analyzing this issue. And I've reached the following conclusion: Italians cannot tolerate being alone. They have to stand next to, touch, be in close proximity to one another. Hence, the need for parallel lines. After all, vertical lines are orderly and orderly lines breed isolation. Nothing interesting comes from orderly lines. Lines that disintegrate before your very eyes, on the other hand, offer splendid opportunities for conversation, laughter, physical contact. Italians must be simultaneously in line and not in line.

The last person in my Coop queue, the woman behind me, has, for example, been insidiously inching forward. Predictably, she now looms near my right shoulder. She is sighing, commenting audibly to herself. It seems clear that she wants to talk to the rest of us, to complain perhaps about the line in which we are all standing, the fast line that isn't so fast. But I'm O.K. with this development. I understand now. She is constitutionally incapable of remaining behind me. She means no harm.

Because I'm unable to put together even a few coherent Italian sentences, the woman begins inching forward once again. Soon, she will appear at the right shoulder of the man in front of me. After awhile, I glance behind me; in our line I see several shoppers, many of whom are waiting along with their twins. I am accustomed to this phenomenon. Still, I can barely resist the urge to snap, "Let's shape up that line, people." Several seconds pass. A new shopper arrives at the end of the line. "*Chi é l'ultima?*" he asks.

Thelma Louise Stiles worked for several decades with the private sector and the federal government before moving to Italy in 1993. Her short stories have appeared in Essence Magazine *and her play is included in the collection,* Center Stage: An Anthology of Twenty-One Contemporary Black-American Plays. *A widow, mother, and granny/nanny, she now lives in Northern California.*

11

PAOLA CORSO

MIRAGE

Didn't the Buddha say that all is illusion?

IT TOOK EXACTLY TWENTY-TWO MINUTES FOR ME, A MOTHER, a daughter, and a dead chicken to board a bus in the Calabrian village of San Procopio. The driver, a slight man with narrow sideburns who was sitting on a bench near the parked bus, appeared to move at a pace that habit had timed for him rather than a schedule. He pulled up his pants, tightened his long belt a notch, and opened the door for me by bumping it a few times with his hip. I handed him money for the ticket, which he accepted graciously as if it were a tip rather than the fare. He bunched it in his shirt pocket with his cigarettes and pointed to all the vacant seats before walking toward the *tabaccaio*. I quickly asked if the bus was going to the *passeggiata* along the water in Reggio Calabria and if it would leave on time. He stared at my money belt before signaling me to board, no doubt thinking I was another tourist in search of the miracle of the Fata Morgana along the Strait of Messina, which meant he knew that I knew that unless he got the bus moving, we'd probably get there too late to witness a fantastic city rising from the sea.

It was a foggy and humid morning, and the odds were as good as they were going to get for the Sicilian town of Messina across the strait to be reflected in the water and air, creating the mirage's rare occurrence. The weather in the afternoon, however, was forecasted to turn sunny as was the remainder of my trip. As much as I enjoyed cooling off in the water, sipping fresh-squeezed lemonade made with the region's Bergamot lemons, and snapping shots of the village with my family's *cugini* under red-tile roofs and blue skies, I came for my mother's Fata Morgana and nothing else.

I made sure the driver saw me tapping on my watch before stepping onto the bus. The rows of empty brown vinyl seats were at perfect right angles, which led me to believe this was once a school bus. The seat cushions were so worn, it felt as though I were sitting in a dried-up mud puddle.

After a few minutes passed and there was still no driver, I waved at him out of my window. He nodded and smiled at me from the *tabaccaio* doorway as he ducked inside the beaded curtain. I sat back down, looked at my watch and worried that my one chance to catch a meteorological freak of nature was ticking away.

I gave him thirty more seconds and then I would get off the bus and fetch him. I'd offer to buy him a gelato and he could lick it while he drove. If he were like other drivers in San Procopio, he'd probably use one hand to steer anyway. Even to navigate the hairpin turns along the steep cliffside to the water.

Just as I was about to hop off the bus, he poked his head outside the curtain of beads at the doorway and shouted, "*Un momentino, signore, per favore.*"

The driver and I obviously had the same difference of opin-

She said it was the testimony of a priest who,
hundreds of years ago, witnessed the Fata Morgana
miracle over the Strait of Messina.

ion over the likelihood of the Fata Morgana that my mother and father had. I remember as a little girl how they would argue. He pulled out the encyclopedia and read what he called scientific fact: "A Fata Morgana mirage is when a layer of hot air traps rays of light coming from distant objects such as rocks, which appear to be towers of a fairy-tale castle. The light rays bend as they pass from the cool, heavy air near the surface to the warm, light air above it."

He slammed the book shut and said that if the Fata Morgana were to occur, which it wouldn't, it was no miracle that it would be in Calabria. "It's got hot air, all right. Not just from the sirocco current from Africa but from all the people down there who have nothing better to do than listen to themselves talk about the Red years and revolution! And there's enough rock in the boot of Italy for a million optical illusions! Ask the *contadini* who work the land. I don't want to hear no more about castles in the sky."

When he walked off, my mother opened the encyclopedia to the page my father read from, his sweaty thumbprint still visible on the corner. She inserted a small piece of onionskin paper with a few sentences handwritten so lightly the Italian words were barely visible. When I asked my mother to read it to me, she said it was the testimony of a priest who, hundreds of years ago, witnessed the Fata Morgana miracle over the Strait of Messina. "The sea, washing up the coast of Sicily, rose up like a dark mountain range. In front of the mountain, a series of white-gray pilasters appeared. Then they shrank to half their height and built arches like those of Roman aqueducts. Castles appeared above the arches, each with towers and windows before it all vanished."

She tucked the thin piece of paper into the encyclopedia as if it were a holy card marking a page in the Bible. In a cadence of prayer, I often heard her reciting it out loud. Her eyes slowly closing, her lips moving ever so slightly, whispering the words so only she could hear them.

One day, thinking the Fata Morgana was visible from the rivers in Pittsburgh because my father was always talking about the confluence at the Point, I asked her if she would take me there to see the miracle.

"Never in Pittsburgh," she insisted, not only because the meteorological conditions weren't right, but Pittsburgh would never take the place of her San Procopio.

My father was just the opposite. Pittsburgh was where he came as a Calabrian orphan and made a life for himself. The city could do no wrong, never mind that he was laid off two years short of collecting a full pension when the steel mills started closing down. Or the bill collectors, the bankruptcies, the loss of a way of life for a class of people. He'd rather be in Pittsburgh over San Procopio. When I'd remind him of the facts, he'd tell me to just go to the Point and look at how the two rivers merge to form a new one. They don't go their separate ways. They come together. That's a miracle every minute of the day.

He hadn't gone back to San Procopio since his uncle brought him to Pittsburgh when his parents died suddenly. When I asked him about it, all he said was that it was an accident. I could tell there was more to it than that, but he didn't want to tell me. No surprise, he thought I was wasting my money by going to San Procopio to look for the Fata Morgana, but before my mother died, she asked me to do one last thing for her, and that was to come here and look for it. Just look for it. It was as if she didn't care if I saw it or not, but that I believed in its possibility. How could I not go and look for it when what I loved most about my mother was how she kept her faith in something despite the improbability? Not just in miracles like the Fata Morgana but in me.

If my father had his way, my best odds for happiness would have been to go to college to be an accountant or a nurse or any occupation that's recession-proof, marry a native Pittsburgher—preferably from a river town—and raise a family there. Take the kids to the Tour-Ed Mine or the Cathedral of Learning for field trips. Pray on Saturdays. Root for the Steelers on Sundays and if there isn't a game, take out-of-town company downtown to ride the incline and view the Point from Mount Washington. But I went to school out of state, got a degree in sociology, live with a man in Queens where the nearest body of water is my neighbor's backed-up rain gutter, and am a self-employed critter sitter who specializes in lucrative play groups for four-legged creatures, and I don't mean a crawling baby. I do pray on Saturdays that I get through another week of auditions and at least get a call back for any part where I have a line.

My mother had no objections to my acting aspirations as long as I could afford to live this way. It was no different than having the money to go to bingo or play the lottery. You have to play to win. She'd pull out her bingo purse filled with dabbers and a magnetic wand to gather her chips every Monday—the only day of the week she was as much of a Pittsburgher as my father.

I hopped off the bus and walked toward the smoke shop. The driver emerged with an elderly woman who had to be twice his weight. She held onto the excess strip of his buckled belt as if it were a leash. Despite walking with a stiff knee, she appeared to be leading him and not vice versa. When they got to the bus, he offered to help her up. She took one step forward as he took two steps back for more leverage to give her a boost from behind. I offered to help, but he assured me in between labored breaths, "Please. No problem."

They finally made it to the first row, but she pitched her purse into the seat behind it. The driver held onto her with one hand and removed the front seat cushion with his other, kicking it to the side. I couldn't imagine why until she sat down and he propped her stiff leg through the metal frame in front of her so she could rest it on the springs.

"*Va bene?*" he asked her.

"*Buono,*" she smiled.

"*Miracolo,*" he said, winking at me as if to say getting her in her seat was more of a spectacle than what I'd see at the Strait of Messina.

I smiled and asked, "*Andiamo, si?*"

The elderly woman moved in her seat to reach for her pocketbook. She handed the man a few coins along with a couple of almonds, then muttered something about waiting for her daughter, although her voice was lost in the swishing sound from all the air trapped inside her seat. He asked if she would need help, too. She shook her head and insisted he sit down.

"*Presto. Presto,*" I pleaded.

He opened his leather pouch and recorded a couple of Roman numerals with a felt-tip pen, making each one slowly and deliberately in calligraphy as if the log were going to be hung on a museum wall next to the *Mona Lisa*. I was ready to ask him if he wanted to borrow the pastel chalks I had in my backpack for drawing but was afraid he'd take me up on it. Already he had to fudge numbers on his schedule because we were more than ten minutes late and the daughter still hadn't boarded the bus. Finally, she arrived, wearing a print skirt that matched her mother's top.

"*Permiso?*" she asked, carrying a live chicken pressed onto her pregnant belly. She got as far as the first step before the driver shook his head, pointing to the chicken.

She stroked the bird and said, "*Per favore, signore.*"

"*No, accommodi,*" he said with a tone of regret.

The bird's yellow eyes began to water. Its feathers lifted with anticipation. Its tail twitched with unease.

When she didn't move, he asked her to leave the chicken outside and reached for the rope to pull the door shut. When she didn't budge, he stepped down to help her decide if she wanted to come in or go out.

He shook his head and turned to her mother. She dropped her stiff leg to the ground and hobbled up the aisle, plopping herself down in the driver's seat. The three of them began clucking louder than the chicken.

I couldn't believe what I saw. There the driver was standing on the bus step: the mother above him, the daughter below, and he in purgatory. I took my watch off and put it in my backpack because I didn't want to know how late we were anymore.

The driver began to shut the door on the daughter, who put the chicken's plumed head between the doors so the driver would stop. He turned to the mother and pleaded with her to help her daughter and the chicken safely off the bus.

"*Aspet,*" the mother ordered. She grabbed onto the rearview mirror and pulled herself up from the driver's seat. She asked her daughter for the chicken. The daughter handed it to the bus driver, who held the bird for a few seconds before insisting that the daughter take the chicken back and leave it behind or she could not get on the bus.

I offered to take the chicken and put it in my backpack so we could go but nobody listened. I poured my things out and handed the driver the empty backpack.

"*No e' necessario*," he said, asking me to please sit back down.

"*Aspet*," the mother said again. This time, she asked the bus driver to hand her the chicken. She would take care of it. He hesitated but before he could give it back to the daughter, the mother snatched the chicken out of his hands, wrapped her chunky fingers around the bird's neck and snapped it like a wishbone.

"*E' morto*," she pronounced as she signaled for the driver to sit in his seat and let her daughter on the bus. The old woman made her way back to her seat, handing me the dead chicken to hold while she sat herself down. She proceeded to prop her leg up on the springs and ask me to give it to her daughter who adjusted her skirt before reaching for the bird. It rested on her belly once again.

The driver was so stunned that he was gripping the wheel but didn't think to start the engine.

The mother looked at her daughter and asked if she was ready. She nodded. Then she looked at me. I nodded. "We go!" she yelled up to the driver and chuckled as I stood and yelled, "*Brava*."

Relieved that everyone was settled and somehow a live animal had not been brought on board, the driver started the bus, letting it drift several yards before he stepped on the gas.

I gathered my things back into my backpack and sat down, eager to enjoy the feeling of motion.

The ride to Reggio was a series of windy, pockmarked roads. The floor of the bus vibrated, and I frequently popped out of my seat like a piece of toast. The women, on the other hand, didn't budge. Even the vineyards on the cliff we drove by somehow defied gravity by rooting themselves in the severe angle of the slope. I couldn't imagine harvesting the grapes there. One false move and it was a long tumble to the sea.

Perhaps I couldn't deny that I had this notion of San Procopio as an isolated corner that couldn't be awakened from its dormancy. That while the rest of the world tossed and turned with restless modernity, this little village slept most of the day.

Not long after we began our journey, the mother pulled out a loaf of bread from her pocketbook. She broke it in half and then half again. She reached inside her purse and put a plump fig on each hunk. She handed one to her daughter and gave me two, signaling for me to take one up to the driver. The bread was so crusty and the fig oozed with sweetness. I wondered how he would manage eating it while he drove, but it seemed to fuel him. After every bite, he hummed and stepped on the gas. As much as I wanted to eat it, I gave him mine.

The bus followed the fishy smell of the sea to the promenade. Even from a distance, I could tell the water was so clear that I imagined dropping a penny and being able to watch it land on the bottom. There were sandy beaches, gritty cement buildings, and eroding castle fortresses. It seemed one wave could wash the city away as though it never existed. I supposed that's what the 1783 and 1908 earthquakes really did. Only the debris wasn't cleared. Instead it mounted, and the city was laid to rest, married to the stone that buried it.

Because natural disasters leveled everything, I hadn't expected Reggio to have old-world charm or even a flavor of each of the rulers who conquered this region, a succession of foreign invasions and feudal order. Greeks. Romans. Normans. French. Spaniards. Arabs. Perhaps I'd see a ruin here or there. Some small fragment but never the whole.

No ivory cupolas rose above the fortress. The skyline was so uniform, not one building could reach upwards from the massive concrete heap weighted down with the rubble of history. The buildings were not what I'd call architecture but rather pale gray shells filled out of necessity. This was my father's Italy. Yet my mother believed this land had something that no earthquake could crumble, no drought could evaporate, no famine could starve, and no plague could wipe out: the hope of seeing the Fata Morgana.

I looked out my window as we approached the promenade to look for believers like my mother. Surely they, too, could feel the cool air near their feet clashing with the warmer air against their faces. I had this idea that there would be rows of occupied benches, all facing the sea. No newspapers. No chatting with friends. No food in their laps. They'd just sit there for hours with their hands folded, watching the sky as if it were an altar.

Instead, it was still quiet from the mid-afternoon siesta. One man, apparently homeless, was using a store window to give himself a mirror for a quick shave. A few people were sitting on the benches but their backs were to the sea. Their expressionless faces reflected the city's mass of petrified stone as though its citizens slept and watched with both eyes closed. Was the Fata Morgana just one more thing from above that would never lower itself to the depths of this city or was the city refusing to lift itself off the ground to rise to the heights of illusion?

I turned to see if the women were looking out their window. The daughter was repositioning the chicken so her mother could feel the kicks in her belly. I smiled and asked if it were a boy or a girl? She laughed and said twins—maybe one of each.

We were approaching my stop. I wanted to ask them if they came to look for the Fata Morgana, but the mother was now examining the chicken, feeling under its feathers and showing the daughter how she would prepare it for dinner that evening.

Before I got off the bus, I took one last look at the lifeless bird resting on a growing belly, its broken neck draped over the daughter's arm. I couldn't help but think of my mother's and father's San Procopio, and wonder if their two worlds would ever meet, if I was waiting for the impossible. But as I glanced out the window at the grit of rubbled buildings and water softened by a light mist, it didn't seem strange at all.

∽

Paola Corso's writing has appeared in The Christian Science Monitor, USA Today, The Progressive, *and* Women's Review of Books. *She is the recipient of the 2000 Sherwood Anderson Fiction Prize. Her story collection,* Giovanna's 86 Circles, *was nominated for a Pushcart Press Editors' Book Award. She is a New York Foundation for the Arts poetry fellow and author of a book of poems,* Death by Renaissance. *She lives in Brooklyn and teaches fiction writing at Fordham University in New York City.*

12

TARAS GRESCOE

ROMAN HOLIDAY

Life imitates art in one of the world's most
fascinating cities.

LEANING AGAINST THE BALCONY ON THE JANICULUM HILLSIDE,
I allow my eyes to sweep from the masts of the Castel
Sant' Angelo to the broken arches of the Colosseum,
taking in what has to be one of the most striking pan-
oramas in Christendom. Rome, Roma, Amor—a place
whose very etymology is linked to romance—is wearing its age well. Newly scrubbed of cinders and exhaust
for the Holy Year, the 2,753-year-old city looks at once
timeless and brand new. Unmarred by office towers,
Space Needles, or Astrodomes, the Roman sky is scraped
only by the tips of Egyptian obelisks, bristling ranks of
freestanding Corinthian columns, and the cupolas of
baroque churches. The view should inspire sober reflec-
tions on the brevity of human life, I suppose, but today,
the catacombs and colonnades seem to whisper only
one question to me: As you live and walk among us,
young man, are you happy?

In other words, I'm ready to fall in love. You see, before

coming to Rome, I made the pleasant mistake of watching *Roman Holiday,* that classic story of abandoning day-to-day responsibilities and unexpected infatuation. Director William Wyler's 1953 tale of a princess from an unnamed nation, playing hooky on a goodwill tour of Europe, comes close to perfection as a romantic comedy, a movie as charmed in the making as it is charming in the watching. It introduced the world to the twenty-four-year-old Audrey Hepburn, a Brussels-born ballet dancer who would win the best actress Academy Award in her first leading role. During the filming, done entirely on location in a postwar Italy mercifully uncluttered by cars, male lead Gregory Peck—playing a cynical newsman for the fictional American News Service—actually fell in love with a French reporter, Veronique Passani, who would become his second wife.

As a carefree jaunt through an enchanting place, *Roman Holiday* sets out a classic itinerary: From the Forum, where Peck first stumbles upon the groggy princess—still reeling from a sedative administered by her doctor, who wanted to make sure she'd have a good night's sleep before her day of appearances—to a café outside the Pantheon, where she has her first cigarette, to the banks of the Tiber, where they dance arm-in-arm, it's a whirlwind city tour by taxi, foot, and scooter.

And so as I watch the cityscape of travertine marble facades beneath me turning honey-toned in the lowering sun, I realize that Rome won't have to work very hard to seduce me. But I also tell myself there has to be a modern-day Audrey Hepburn out there, idly sipping espresso in one of those piazzas—somebody willing to give up a day to help me with an ephemeral tour of an eternal city.

But before I can seek her out, I need to get my bearings. I'd been prepared for a Rome smudged with exhaust, choked with cars, and overrun by tour buses. But what I find is a highly walkable city, its Bernini fountains and Michelangelo-designed palazzos newly cleansed of centuries of pollution, and, thanks to the initiatives of the mayor, its narrowest streets served by quietly humming electric buses the size of milk vans.

The Centro Storico, the ancient core whose cavernous streets compensate for their gloom by breaking into sun-flooded piazzas, is now a patchwork of pedestrians-only zones. Lurching chains of riverside traffic can still make crossing to the bohemian Trastevere neighborhood or Vatican City a trial, but from footbridges like Ponte Sisto, the shores of the serpentine Tiber, dotted with fishermen's poles and families of ducks, seem oddly bucolic.

I also have the time to make a few simple observations. First: Everybody here—priest, lawyer, ticket taker—seems to own a cell phone and uses it all the time. (They are more reliable, I learn, than the standard phone system.) Second: Italians really do talk with their hands. Unfortunately, they also drive with their cell phones. Which means that, torn as they are between gesticulating and steering, Roman drivers are now the most lethal in Europe. Finally, the citizens of Rome are a real oddity in Europe: They seem to take genuine pleasure in their jobs and lives, and actually appear to enjoy the presence of outsiders. (At least the ones they haven't run over.)

I spend my first two days roaming the city's streets in a happy daze, eating my first Roman pizza—whose crêpe-thin crust miraculously supports eggplant, sausage, and bitter greens—and drinking espresso unmolested by that barman's scowl that is de rigueur in Paris and London.

Rome, I'm also beginning to notice, is full of lithe and mysterious-looking women, many of whom could pass for errant princesses. I audition my first Audrey at a café terrace in the Trastevere neighborhood, striking up a conversation with an elegantly dressed stranger in dark sunglasses who's reading a Paul

Auster novel over a cappuccino. Her name is Francesca, and she turns out to be an Italian ballerina who trained with the Bolshoi; what's more, she remembers seeing *Roman Holiday*—or *Vacanze Romane,* as it is known here—as a child, and loving it. When I invite her on a city tour, she not only agrees, but also invites me for drinks that night—and as I arrive, she immediately presents me to her scowling, broad-shouldered beau. The next morning, ensconced in the red velvet banquettes of the Antico Caffè Greco, where we'd agreed to meet, I'm not particularly surprised when she fails to keep the date. Francesca, I pout, has definitely failed the audition. Audrey Hepburn would never have resorted to such an elaborate ruse simply to make a boyfriend jealous.

Via Margutta was a tax-free zone for foreigners in the fifteenth and sixteenth centuries—Caravaggio lived here. And more recently, Fellini did, too.

Ah well, I muse, bucking myself up with every cliché in the book: Rome is the capital of the world, so when all roads lead to Rome (a city, they tell me, that was not built in a day), you might as well do as the Romans do.

I decide to try my luck on the Spanish Steps, that curving staircase that cascades down from the Trinità dei Monti church, home to a permanent population of teenage boys inspecting the girls who are inspecting the lingerie at the Dolce & Gabbana store. Sandwiched between the Keats-Shelley Memorial House and Babington's Tea Rooms, named after the nearby Spanish embassy to the Vatican, and a favorite photo-op for Japanese shoppers, the Steps are about as cosmopolitan a setting as you can find in Rome.

It was here, at the Spanish Steps, that Gregory Peck's character—hiding his identity as a newsman eager for a scoop—urged

Audrey Hepburn to eat gelati, and "take a little time for yourself...
live dangerously." Giggling, Hepburn gets into the spirit of the
city: "I'd like to do just whatever I like the whole day long.... Sit
at a sidewalk café, and look in shop windows, walk in the rain—
have fun, and maybe some excitement. It doesn't seem much to
you, does it?"

Certainly not to me, anyway.

The rain has stopped, Rome is throbbing all around me, and
I decide to take a chance, sitting down next to a pretty young
woman with wavy black hair in a mauve sweater, who's been absorbed by an Italian translation of *Madame Bovary* for the last half
hour. Ten minutes of fast talking later, I have my Audrey.

Her name is Elisabetta—a good name for a monarch's stand-
in, I figure—she's from Naples, and when I describe my plan, she
sighs: "Ah, *Vacanze Romane!*" in gratifying recognition. "I loved
[she says this word in two syllables] this film." In town for a job
interview, Elisabetta has three spare hours ahead of her, and she
giggles with a hint of Hepburn's spontaneity when I warn her
that my Italian is as sketchy as her English seems to be shaky.

"Is no important," she says, standing up and brushing off her
pants, "*Andiamo!*"

I remind Elisabetta of the movie's plot as we walk toward our
first stop, the setting for Peck's bachelor pad. The reporter, weary
after a night of poker-playing, reluctantly takes the sleepy princess back to his apartment—after unsuccessfully trying to fob
her off on a taxi driver by waving a Kleenex-size 5,000-lire note.

The straight-backed Hepburn, unimpressed by Peck's
cramped digs, blearily inquires, "Is this the elevator?"

In fact, Paramount's location scouts had chosen one of Rome's
best addresses, the enviably situated Via Margutta. Even today,
though the street is only about a hundred yards away from traffic
chaos and Armani, Chanel, and other designer emporia, it feels

very much like a three-block-long transplant from Paris's Montmartre, an unexpected, welcome oasis of tranquility that backs up toward the quiet park paths of the tree-lined Pincio hillside.

Feeling giddy as teenage trespassers, Elisabetta and I walk through the tall carriage entrance that leads to the gravel-strewn courtyard of Via Margutta, 51. I instantly recognize the setting—we're at the entrance to the staircase, overhung by a slanted, vine-covered arbor, where the princess is forced to borrow cab fare after she wakes up in Peck's apartment.

This is clearly an idiosyncratic little enclave, filled with painters' studios, well-fed cats, and stray sculptures. In vague hopes of finding the apartment that was Peck's in *Roman Holiday,* we rap on the door to a movie production-company called Cineroma.

"Come in," says a man sitting behind a laptop computer in an open, loft-like studio. He introduces himself as David Nichols, and it turns out he's an American-born, British-raised executive producer who fell in love with Italy and decided to settle down and work from Rome.

"This is a unique place," Nichols says, leaning back in his chair. "It's very quiet. When you wake up in the morning you hear the birds. It's one of the oldest sections of Rome, and a great community of artists used to live here. Via Margutta was a tax-free zone for foreigners in the fifteenth and sixteenth centuries—Caravaggio lived here. And more recently, Fellini did, too."

Nichols adds, just a little ruefully, that it was only after he moved in that he learned William Wyler's film had been made here. "*Roman Holiday* seems to be big in Japan, so we regularly get scores of Japanese tourists coming into the courtyard." (From upstairs, his wife, Jenny, shouts, "More like hundreds of them.")

Outside, I ask Elisabetta if she expected to find a place like Via Margutta in the heart of Rome. "Oh, is nice," she says grudgingly, "but we have many places in Napoli like this." Hmmm—

I'd heard tell of this Neapolitan pride, born of an age-old rivalry between Rome and Naples. Back on the street, we stroll among art galleries and antique shops in seventeenth-century buildings, until Elisabetta grabs my arm and shouts, "Gregorio!" She's spotted a poster for *Roman Holiday* in the window of the Osteria Margutta.

The restaurant is closed until dinner, but we talk to an employee who's setting up a buffet. "I can tell you that Gregory Peck* has been here this year," says waitress Valeria Testarmata, setting down a plate of roasted red, yellow, and green peppers. "He didn't want to speak about himself as an actor. He just came and sat here, because he saw the poster outside. He said everything was like it was so many years ago; nothing has changed."

I think I know what he meant. In spite of the cell phones and high-tech Smart cars, Rome's fundamental pleasures seem reassuringly eternal, as though the Romans—whether they're senators in sandals or techno kids in platform shoes—have always been strolling these same cobblestones, enjoying guiltless gelati and sunshine.

Inspired by Audrey Hepburn's example, Elisabetta and I make a pit stop for ice cream, pausing at Il Gelato di San Crispino, an ice cream parlor that's generally considered to be the best in Rome, if not in Italy. The paper-hatted counterman gives me my scoop of zabaglione, made with egg yolks and Marsala and served in a cup (an artificially flavored cone, the owners claim, would compromise the purity of the experience).

We take our booty to the steps in front of the Trevi Fountain, that baroque fantasy of finned horses surging from beneath a billowy-bearded Neptune, crammed into a piazza so tiny it suggests *The Tempest* being performed in a teapot.

* Peck died in 2003 at the age of 87.

I ask Elisabetta whether her scoop—she's ordered the epony-
mous house specialty, whose creamy yellowish tint comes from
traces of Sardinian wild honey—is as good as what she gets back
home. "Is O.K.," she concedes, "but the gelato in Napoli is very
good, too." It seems I'm dealing with an unbeatable case of civic
pride.

While I'm debating whether it's worth asking if she prefers
thick-crusted Neapolitan pizza to its thinner Roman counterpart, she looks at her watch, jumps up, and cries "O, *Dio*!"

It's time for her job interview; like Audrey Hepburn in the
film, Elisabetta is being beckoned by reality. I wish her luck, but
before we go, we have to engage in the official Trevi Fountain cer-
emony.

Turning our backs to the fountain, we toss coins over our
shoulders. My wish, I tell her, is to come back to Rome—next
time, with a significantly better command of Italian. Elisabetta,
however, her coin sinking to the robin's-egg-colored bottom, refuses to tell me hers.

"When you throw," she giggles, "you must make a wish, but
you cannot tell what it was. *Capito?*" *Capito*, I say, a little sad. We
exchange kisses on the cheeks, and she runs off with a wave, leaving me to wonder whether her wish featured me or Gregory Peck
in the leading role.

Alone, but not lonely—it's hard to feel abandoned in this
intensely social city—I decide to complete my *Roman Holiday* itinerary on the back of a scooter. Tearing a garage owner away from
his soccer game, I rent a Yamaha, a little disappointed not to get
the Vespa of my dreams. ("It's maybe Japanese," he consoles me,
shooing a cat off the seat, "but motor is a Minarelli.") Soon, I'm
juddering over cobblestones, slipping between lines of cars, and
circling the Colosseum, where muscle men in gladiators' capes
wield plastic swords and pose for tourist photos. Then I drive past

the Forum, that ancient civic center turned quarry, where director William Wyler was delighted to learn that guides had started telling tourists: "Here is where Caesar is buried. On those steps is where Marc Antony spoke. And over here is where Audrey Hepburn and Gregory Peck played a scene in *Roman Holiday*."

Outside the Vatican walls, I roar onto a quiet street—which turns out to be a pedestrian zone—and am pointed toward the curb by a *carabiniere*. Rather than interrupt his conversation with two colleagues, however, he uses some impressively expressive mime to indicate I should turn off my motor and simply walk my scooter to the end of the pedestrian zone. Near the Castel Sant' Angelo, a schooner-like fortress that for centuries sheltered popes from marauding barbarians, I pause just long enough to note that the riverbank where the princess and the newsman danced on a moored barge for the first and last time is now utterly bare.

Finally, I use my scooter to make a special pilgrimage, to a church called Santa Maria. It was here that Gregory Peck stuck his hand into the slit-mouthed Bocca della Verità, a circular relief of a hirsute god (actually an ancient drain cover), eliciting an unscripted cry of alarm from Audrey Hepburn when he pulled his arm out of the hole with his hand tucked up his sleeve.

As I take off my helmet, I see the church's portico is full of people lining up to have their pictures taken in front of the antique manhole. Two Japanese girls enter, and one of them leaps in the air in delight when she sees the familiar face. To her alarm, however, a squat Italian man in his fifties grabs her wrist and thrusts it into the gaping mouth, pushing her sleeve up over her hand in imitation of Gregory Peck as he pulls it out. "*Vacanze Romane!*" he cries in triumph.

Later that day, buzzing beneath aqueducts on the Janiculum hilltop at sunset, I realize that it's finally happened: I've fallen in love. Not with any ringer for Audrey Hepburn (although Elisabetta had a certain winsome charm...) but with Rome itself. It has to be love, because I forgive Rome for everything, even her traffic. I forgive the woman on the Lambretta scooter in the swank Aventino neighborhood, who, driving with one hand on the throttle, the other on her cell phone, almost ran me over. I admire the élan of the guys who drive up onto the sidewalks, not bothering to dismount from their motorbikes to withdraw money from wall-mounted bank machines. And I out-and-out love a place where I've seen flocks of nuns power-shopping in religious knickknack stores on the Borgo Pio, or teenage boys presenting a middle-aged woman on the Spanish Steps with a single spray-painted rose.

At the tear-wrenching end of *Roman Holiday,* Audrey Hepburn shows her regal mettle by returning to her life as a princess. In turn, Gregory Peck demonstrates his class by returning to the daily grind, resisting the temptation to turn his romantic outing into a scoop. Happily, I've got no such motivation to deny myself a newfound love. Forget noble self-restraint: I fully intend to return to Rome, and I've got a quarter in the Trevi Fountain that says it's going to be soon.

Taras Grescoe is the author of The Devil's Picnic: Around the World in Pursuit of the Forbidden Fruit, The End of Elsewhere: Travels Among the Tourists, *and* Sacre Blues: An Unsentimental Journey Through Quebec. *His work also appears in major magazines and newspapers in North America.*

13

SNAPPING OUT
OF IT IN NAPLES

It is good to be reminded of your origins.

ONE OF MY FAVORITE MOVIE MOMENTS IS IN *MOONSTRUCK* when Nicholas Cage tells Cher he loves her, she slaps him and barks, "Snap out of it!" It reminds me of the no-holds-barred passion I grew up with. Like *Moonstruck*, my childhood on the Jersey Shore was full of first generation immigrants from southern Italy— those folks who brought to America great things like pizza, *sfogliatelle*, and my personal favorite: high-volume emotional outbursts.

It's a behavior style I never see in Los Angeles. Here, if a guy says "I love you" right after he meets you, the gal smiles sweetly and suggests medication. That's why it was so refreshing to go to the source of the noisy passion I was weaned on: Naples, Italy.

It was all so familiar from the moment I hit the street. There they were: look-alikes of those broad expressive faces and hands flying through the air that entertained me as a kid.

At the café, I order a cappuccino and *bam*! Even before my milk is steamed, the show begins with shouts of "No, no!" from the café owner. He waves his arms in protest against a pleading gentleman in a suit. Signore Suit simply wants to leave something behind the counter: a live wriggling eel. The eel, after all, is in a bag; he'd just bought it from the fish cart outside. Thick open-palmed "No" hands debate pinched *"Per favore"* fingers. Nothing like my quiet L.A. Starbucks, where hands only move to click laptops and cell phones.

And I definitely know I'm not in Los Angeles when I get to the park and there are no mommies calmly offering their children choices: "Kyle you can either get in the car immediately or have a time out." No—here in the Piazza Communale exasperated mammas yell, *"Aldo, vieni qua!"* Aldo keeps kicking his soccer ball until mamma grabs him by the collar and drags him to the bus.

Later, at the trattoria, our waiter, Marco stands at my table and bellows: "Spaghetti, gnocchi!" He's not angry, just passionate about pasta. This is no Beverly Hills lunch spot, where waiters whisper specials like "Pan-seared Ahi Tuna over Papaya Coulis," as if it were a rare disease.

Outside, I join a crowd gathered for a puppet show starring Pucinella, the mascot of Naples. We watch that rascal clown declare his love for a wide-eyed *signorina* puppet. Pucinella goes in for a kiss, she grabs a baseball bat and whacks poor "Puch" mercilessly. It's the cartoon version of Cher's "Snap out of it" *Moonstruck* slap. As we all laugh, a teenager on a Vespa bursts through the crowd to speed down an alley. All us startled grown-ups lift our arms: *"Ay!"*

I catch my reflection in a bakery window. That's me: framed by *baba* and *sfogliatelle*, hands raised, mouth open, with all the other five-foot-tall, olive-skinned ladies. I've become a member of the chorus in the land of my ancestors. It feels *fantastico* to snap out of it.

⌒◯

Susan Van Allen is a Los Angeles-based writer who has written for many publications and media outlets, including public radio's "Savvy Traveler" and "Marketplace," CNN.com, and the television show Everybody Loves Raymond. *She travels to Italy as often as possible to visit relatives, eat and drink well, bike through the countryside, wander through museums, and enjoy the flirtations of those handsome Italian men.*

14

SEAN O'REILLY

ST. PETER'S BLACK BOX*

An apostate stumbles upon a secret.

STAND BEFORE THE PLAZA IN FRONT OF ST. PETER'S BASILICA in Rome and let it impose itself on your imagination. As you gaze at the religious center of 2,000 years of creative and passionate spiritual endeavor, you may feel a touch of humility. Here in the presence of the unthinkable successor to the mighty Roman Empire, consciousness tends to implode, to shift into reverie and things besides mere thoughts enter the mind. So much history in one place creates a time warp where the collective consciousness of untold generations invades your synapses and leaves the vision slightly blurred to accommodate the intrusion. One staggers through this psychic doorway to discover that nothing is as it seems.

* A black box in science fiction is anything for which the reader has to suspend reality.

I was a second year student in the University of Dallas Rome program. We were allowed to spend three days in class and the rest of the week roaming Europe. Students went just about everywhere—Paris, the coast of Spain, Germany, Austria, Switzerland, and even North Africa, but it was in Rome that I discovered something so unusual that the experience has stayed with me for nearly thirty-five years.

The first thing I noticed after entering the Basilica on that sunny day, was the confessional lights—bright against the dark, almost blackened wood—then the signs in many languages above the confessional boxes. They seemed forbidding and ritual-encrusted, like an archaic technology left over from a vanished yet still vital world.

Confessions were being heard in Spanish, English, Chinese, Malay, Polish, Czech, Russian, and God knows how many other tongues. I thought to myself, "How convenient, anyone could go." Immediately, I countered with the thought that it would be convenient for those who *wanted* to go—myself of course not being included. I could not tear myself away, however, and for some reason I kept looking at the lights. I forcibly walked the other way, thinking that there should be many other more interesting things to look at. I wandered over to the Pieta and marveled at the flow of the marble. Only the real masters were able to make marble look like human flesh. (The work of Praxiteles came to mind and the stunning statue of Antinous at Delphi—small wonder that Hadrian had been so captivated by him.)

After a few minutes with Michelangelo, I found myself back in the same place. I started to become annoyed. What bullshit! Who could need confession? I was surprised that this was even an issue for me, as I had left the Catholic Church at fourteen and at twenty-one had no intention of returning. I was suddenly caught in the gravitation of the struggle that was going on and recognized that I was, in fact, having an argument with my spiritual self. It was one of those rare moments when you catch yourself looking at yourself and wondering what the problem really is. From this illumined perspective, desires whether for good or ill are transparently clear. You either want something or you do not. I experienced what in retrospect might be called a paradigm shift. I found myself denying what appeared to be a bizarre desire (from my perspective at the time) and simultaneously realized from an entirely different and larger perspective that what I wanted was tantalizing and possibly beneficial in a way I could not understand.

I knew at that point that I had to go into the confessional; there was no honest way out. I simply wanted to go and there was no denying it. I felt a subtle shuddering as if I was standing at the edge of a cliff and there was no turning back. At the same time there was an immense and pending clarity to what I was about to do. The fulfillment of my own history, a venture into the unknown, a vast quantum leap into the future seemed to be at hand. I hesitated; what sins would I confess? The answer bore down on me with awful certainty: "confess all of them." I realized that if I was going to go through with this, there was no point in doing it halfway.

So I went in and confessed all my misdeeds from age fourteen to twenty-one, a seven-year accumulation of sexual misconduct and a host of other failings. I do not remember all that I confessed or even what the priest was like but I do remember stumbling out of the confessional like a person facing a new dawn after a reprieve from some long incarceration. I felt lighter and also re-oriented—as if something had been out of focus and was now much clearer. I immediately wrote it off to psychological relief but could not quite escape the sense that something extraordinary had happened.

My life was never the same after that. I had many moral lapses from that day on but always went back to "the box" for confession, and astoundingly, the relief from spiritual oppression and darkness always seemed to occur. If I had to describe it another way, I would say that before I go to confession, I feel fragmented, vaguely depressed, somewhat inverted, and upon receiving the forgiveness of the priest, set aright or made joyfully whole in a mysterious manner. The suspension of the literal mind that is required to confess indicates to me that St. Peter's Black Box may open a doorway onto a different reality. The experience brings to mind Robert Heinlein's fabulous science fiction title, *The Door into Summer*. For me, such a door was a spiritual gateway to the future.

Sean O'Reilly is director of special sales and editor-at-large for Travelers'
Tales. He is a former seminarian, stockbroker, and prison instructor who lives in
Virginia with his wife Brenda and their six children. He's had a lifelong interest
in philosophy, theology, and travel, and is the author of How to Manage
Your DICK: Redirect Sexual Energy and Discover Your More
Spiritually Enlightened, Evolved Self *(www.dickmanagement.com). His*
most recent travels have taken him through China, Thailand, Indonesia, the South
Pacific, and Malaysia.

15

BANANA TOWER

Yes, you do need to see it, and yes,
it is worth the visit.

When I was young, my father bounced me on his
knee, reciting the words to a rhyme in a hushed and
tuneless monotone.

> Paris has la Tour Eiffel
> Babylon had its tower as well
> But neither has the power to *seize ya*
> Like the Leaning Tower of Pisa.

Every time he got to *seize ya,* he grabbed my shoulders
and squeezed, and I shrieked in a confusion of fear and
delight.

Dad taught high school physics and astronomy, and
my bedtime stories often featured such heroes as Copernicus, Borelli, and da Vinci. And Galileo. How bold Galileo seemed, overturning Aristotle and challenging the
Inquisition! How brilliant his mind, to invent the telescope, discover the moons of Jupiter, and develop elegant
theories of periodic motion. How many times I imagined

him standing at the top of that famous bell tower in Pisa, holding a cannon ball in one hand and a wooden ball in the other, poised to demonstrate the laws of gravitational acceleration.

Pisa infused my imagination for years: art, science, and religion, steeped through time, reappearing at occasional lucky moments in TV specials and history books, in art classes, and in my dreams. It reminded me of my father, and of great men throughout history; in my young psyche, the city came to represent civilization itself. I longed to see the Santa Maria della Spina, a gorgeous, three-spired gothic church that houses a single thorn from Christ's crown. Christ's blood surely must have permeated that thorn, must have been part of it for more than two thousand years, must still be part of it at this very moment. Campo Santo gave me the shivers: a graveyard containing dirt the Crusaders brought back from the Holy Land, filled with crumbling sarcophagi—some of which had been used over and over again. Imagine the jumble of dirt and DNA, memories and history, ghosts and skeletons there! And I wanted to visit the Arsenale, where the remains of more than fifteen ships are skeletons, too, their well-preserved ribs protruding unmistakably from ancient silt, recalling Pisa's glory days as a wealthy seaport.

More than anything, I wanted to climb the Leaning Tower of Pisa. Built over the course of two hundred years, the fact that the tower leaned was evident early on. Builders attempted to rectify the situation by constructing the tower itself on a compensatory slant, and the result is a subtle but definite banana-shaped curve. As a child, I thought of it as the Banana Tower.

Many times I had imagined myself in Pisa, holding my father's hand, wandering intimate, arcaded streets, then strolling across the manicured Field of Miracles—a stately central lawn—toward a wildly tilting Banana Tower. I didn't know *why* the surrounding area was called the Field of Miracles, but I supposed the Virgin

> Eight hundred years ago, children just like me had
> entered the tower and shuddered at the *animali*
> *mostruosi*—monstrous animals—then hurried up the
> steps to the comfort of plain limestone block walls.

had appeared to someone there. That, or an innocent baby had been cured of a horrible disease. Perhaps both, since it was called the Field of Miracles—plural. The sky radiated bright blue (it never rained in my imagination), the grass rolled out a perfect, verdant carpet (despite the lack of rain), and the bright sun reflecting off white marble nearly blinded me. The Banana Tower's cool, curved interior beckoned in welcome relief.

Escaping the heat of the day, I would enter a world of fantastic animals, with monsters and sea battles and hog-bears circling around me, no less frightening because they were captured in stone. Eight hundred years ago, children just like me had entered the tower and shuddered at the *animali mostruosi*—monstrous animals—then hurried up the steps to the comfort of plain limestone block walls, punctuated only by the sunlight streaming in at each narrow window. We climbed the tower many times, those children and I, all 294 steps. I still remember that odd hog-bear from one of my childhood picture books; I remember the serpents and the battleships sailing on wiggly waves as though I had seen them myself.

I had dreamed many times of visiting the Pisa of my childhood imagination, and now, twenty-three years later, I was climbing the stairs of the famous Leaning Tower. Even though I *knew* it would not look much like a banana, and would not be filled with the delicious banana aroma I had imagined as a child, I was still mildly disappointed. There were only a few animal sculptures at the base of the monument, and they were smaller than I had expected. After I'd rounded the central column three times, I felt pleasantly off-kilter. But by the fifth, the combination of close quarters, physical exertion, a dizzying tilt, and pushing tourists conspired to make me reconsider my plan to reach the top. Not only were the stairs themselves slanted, they were also deeply worn—from the footsteps of millions of visitors during the past eight centuries—and maintaining my balance became increasingly difficult. The alternating darkness and bright sunlight made my head ache, and I thought the view from the top of the tower was probably not as exhilarating as I had previously imagined. What sense was there in continuing, only to be disappointed? But the crowd behind me was insistent; it became a sinuous sea serpent, pushing me upward and devouring all hope of escape.

At the top, fresh air and an expansive view rejuvenated me. The Baptistery far below looked like a giant wedding cake, creamy white and layered and voluptuous, with its egg-like dome. The vast piazza was hemmed with an exuberant string of souvenir stalls, and beyond that stretched ochre-tiled rooftops, narrow streets, medieval palaces, and the winding Arno River.

Ah, the Arno. Wide and lazy, it is a placid reflectory for the noble *palazzos* lining its banks. Perhaps silk merchants had lived in these palaces, presiding over open-air markets here at the end of the exotic Silk Road, which once stretched all the way to China. Surely they strolled across the Ponte di Mezzo, enjoying the afternoon breeze and picnicking on salty olives and pungent pecorino.

I was beginning to imagine Galileo standing beside me—I would happily hold the cannon ball for him, my father would join us—and could have continued my medieval reverie indefinitely, but our guide indicated that the group must descend.

Tours were tightly scheduled, and I had time for just one last look from the Leaning Tower. Tourists in the piazza below assumed the I'm-holding-up-the-tower pose—arms outstretched, one leg bent—for their companions with cameras. Cliché, but I couldn't help smiling along with them. *Click.* "O.K., now *you* hold it up and I'll take the photo, then we've got to catch the bus." *Click.* A crowd was gathering for the next tour. Souvenir vendors hawked their wares: miniature towers, books and postcards, tea towels and salt-and-pepper sets, keychains, plastic skulls and lizards—reminders of the Campo Santo.

"*Andiamo!* Time to go!" Was this what Pisa had become? Tourists herded from one attraction to another, planning their day around the bus schedule, rushed into and out of the Leaning Tower, purchasing silly plastic mementos destined to gather dust on faraway bookshelves? My heart sank in bitter disappointment: science and religion had abandoned this place. Romance, beauty, and history had deserted; civilization had fled. Had it been this way for ten years, or for one hundred? Did my father know? Had he known all along?

I looked more closely.

A gray-haired couple, well-dressed and holding hands, emerged from the Duomo, admiring its intricate, multicolored stonework: mosaic stars, complex geometric patterns, long, calm bands of gray-green marble. Unhurried, they ambled toward the Baptistery, stopping to watch a flock of pigeons pecking at the grass.

Nearby, a woman about my age sat on a bench. Her face was flushed, and I thought her feet must be tired, because a pair of black, high-heeled sandals sat on the bench beside her. On the woman's lap was a small child, barely old enough to sit by itself, but already with a headful of the kind of fine blond hair that looks like cornsilk, and sparkles in the sunshine. I wondered whether this child, too, had heard stories of Galileo and Copernicus, of ancient sailors and the moons of Jupiter.

Slowly, the woman began to bounce her knees, and her child squealed in delight. I couldn't hear the woman's words, but I knew my father's rhyme by heart:

> Paris has la Tour Eiffel
> Babylon had its tower as well
> But neither has the power to *seize ya*
> Like the Leaning Tower of Pisa.

Laurie McAndish King has celebrated New Years' Eve in Venezuela, chased lemurs through the rainforests of Madagascar, tracked lions—on foot and without a gun—in Botswana, and survived a kidnapping in Tunisia. Her story about locking her keys in the car in the middle of the Australian Outback appears in the Travelers' Tales volume The Thong Also Rises. *Laurie publishes an online newsletter for travel writers (www.laurieking.com), indulges her passions for natural history, anthropology, and travel, and occasionally dreams about the Banana Tower.*

16

GEORGIA I. HESSE

BLISTERS IN PARADISE

It's a walk she won't soon forget,
through the Italy of fantasies.

ONCE UPON A TIME THERE WERE FIVE LANDS AND YOU couldn't get there from here. They were named, from north to south, Monterosso, Vernazza, Corniglia, Manarola, and Riomaggiore. They perched like afterthoughts above Italy's wild Ligurian coast and were called, collectively, the Cinque Terre (Five Lands). They had been around forever but we had heard of them only last Thursday.

Ken, Dariel, and I lunched outdoors at Taverna del Marinaio by the harbor in Portofino, our chairs creaking companionably on the cobbles. We ate strands of *spaghetti vongole* and toasted the golden day with the red wine of the house. The afternoon stretched out like a lazy dog.

As the sun sank, it seemed time to motor south, in search of some place small and cozy to sleep. Somehow, we found ourselves at the menacing, black mouth of a tunnel, stuck at a red light. We waited, cool with contentment, as the minutes idled by and cars stacked up behind us.

Then it was our turn. The light greened and we plunged into the tortuous tunnel that takes you to Moneglia and, if you survive, to the Cinque Terre.

Narrow, black, rough-walled as a mine, our burrow bore through the very bowels of earth. Faster, faster, deeper, deeper, we careened around inky blind curves, pursued by mad Italians: We were Alice, falling down the rabbit hole, and we giggled wildly like children in a fun house.

We exited from Middle Earth in Moneglia, where the Locanda Maggiore hotel graciously accepted us despite its closed-for-the-season sign.

Next day, in more sober but still antic style, we motored the few kilometers to Monterosso and settled, sighing with satisfaction, into the forty-three-room Porto Roca overhanging the Ligurian Sea. On the horizon, green mountains climbed away toward Genoa.

In Monterosso, the medieval Aurora tower stands on an outcrop called Cappuccini and divides the new town from the old. Small, sheltered, and isolated Monterosso may be, but flyers everywhere announced the concert of a choir and orchestra from Lerici, bragged of a symphony from London.

We lunched on delicacies brought straight from the sea to Pensione R. Moretto and learned to like the local wine, Sciacchetra. (A handful of years later, my mother would dub it Scratchy Terra, which elegantly defines its earthy essence.)

What one is expected to do in the Cinque Terre is to take the little train (one Prince Albert might have designed to carry guests from London out to the Crystal Palace) from the village of Monterosso (the first "land") to Riomaggiore (the fifth) in about twelve minutes and to spend the rest of the day hiking back via the pastel aeries of Vernazza, Corniglia and Manarola. The train cuts through the cliffs (as Ken, the artist, put it) like an arrow shot through a pleated skirt.

The ancient houses of Riomaggiore stand on each other's shoulders in a narrow valley sliced by streams. Houses in pink, houses in grey, houses in homely indiscriminate shades are fronted with green shutters battened against the brilliance of the sea-reflected sun.

We inspected the local church; we bought fresh, still-warm grapes by the bunch from a woman with relatives in the Bronx; we stepped out along the panoramic parade that leads to Manarola.

So far, so smooth: a mere amble, we agreed it was as we reached Manarola. Too bad it is too early to stop for lunch at the Marina Piccola with its seductive seafood odors. But we have our Sciacchetra, our *pane* and *formaggio* and a local sausage, so let's carry on to Corniglia.

My notes are nonexistent after Manarola. I have no record of the surfeit of steps that climb from the sea toward the piazza in Corniglia, no hint of the hot-dust path we plodded steeply up and always up, no note of the nagging weight of cameras or of our collapse in the blessed shade of an olive grove from which we gazed back at the wicked way we had come.

As we swilled the Sciacchetra, all the dogs in the village below burst into barks, quieted only when Ken broke into manic operatic voice. It would never go at La Scala, but it certainly silenced Cinque Terre.

"Open my heart and you shall see/ Graven inside of it — Italy." Lord Byron's ghost spoke in the grove.

When you have trudged so far, there is no way back, no way out. You have committed to stumbling on. Our track (I think now we were on the wrong one) had left the sea and wound up, around, up to a miniscule settlement not on our map. The remains of the day are a blur, a haze, a veil of images. We had become as stubborn and uncaring and mindless as mules.

Somewhere en route, I became a medieval European, laboring leagues from walled town to walled town only to arrive after sunset to find the city gates locked.

In the woods above Vernazza, the second "land," Dariel dropped into the autumn leaves. "Ken," she almost sobbed, "go on. And tell the boys I've always loved them."

While Ken debated, I scurried into the village and into a bar so when the two wearies staggered from the shadows I (with the aid of an amused bartender) was waiting in the middle of the short street with a table, three chairs, and three chilled beers.

Twilight flickered on. The will said mush, you huskies. But the feet failed. Darkness approached and so did a train. We boarded it.

Back on our terrace at Porta Roca, we drank everything at hand, displayed our wounds to each other, heroes escaped from the wars. No one can know the trouble we'd seen: glory, hallelujah.

Once upon a time, I walked from the fifth to the second land. Once upon another time, I will make it to the first.

∽͡ᗒ

Georgia I. Hesse, founding travel editor of the San Francisco Examiner Chronicle, *has visited and written about 199 countries and island groups.*

17

MARCY GORDON

SCIOPERO!

It's a word known to strike fear into the hearts of travelers.

REMEMBER THAT SCENE IN *THE GRADUATE* WHEN DUSTIN Hoffman's character Benjamin is pulled aside at a cocktail party and a guy says to him "I'm going to tell you the one most important word you need to know for the future—"Plastics"— well in Italy the most important word you need to know is *"Sciopero"*— Strike!

I learned the word the hard way while I was attending the Università per Stranieri in Perugia, Italy.

In my class I met and became friends with a young woman from China named Claudia. Claudia and her friends couldn't understand why someone twice their age would be studying Italian with them. But they were very sweet, treating me with great affection as if I were a Chia pet that needed tending. They were all very studious, and we could only speak to each other in Italian. Yet within a week I convinced Claudia to ditch class and go to Florence for the day. I told Claudia that we would buy her the most expensive leather coat we can find at the market in Florence and put it on her father's credit card. This intrigued and horrified her at the same time, but nonetheless, she agreed to meet me at the train station the following day for our trip.

We arrived at the station at 7:30 A.M. to catch our 8:00 A.M. train only to find a general strike had been called until 4:00 P.M. There was mass confusion as hundreds of displaced travelers mulled about the station trying to figure out what to do. With no other transportation options available for Florence, we decided to head back to town and go to class as usual. We pushed into the ubiquitous blob of people that passes as a line in Italy and merged and squeezed our way on to the number 16 bus bound for Piazza Italia.

I asked Claudia if we were on the right bus, and she answered "Yes, don't worry." So I didn't—who was I to doubt a twenty-three-year-old from Shanghai? Once the crush of passengers lightened up we were able to get seats in the back. We passed several landmarks and then it appeared that we were headed out of town, not into it. I asked Claudia again if we were on the right bus, but this time her answer was not so confident. "*Non so.*" "I don't know," she said. Things were not looking familiar anymore. Claudia assured me it was just a different route and we would eventually arrive at Piazza Italia. So I decided to sit back, relax, and enjoy the view.

After a few more stops the bus was almost empty. Nothing looked familiar now and once the last person exited the bus at a

We walked to the front of the bus and asked the driver what was going on. He seemed surprised to see us and gave us the dead-eye stare.

desolate looking crossroads, the bus driver accelerated at a break-neck speed and we went careening down the road in the opposite direction of town. Way out of town. I wondered if the driver even knew we were on board, but he was driving so fast I was afraid to stand up and ask where we were going.

Finally, near a fairground, the driver pulled over, stopped the bus, lit a cigarette, put his feet up on the wheel, and began reading the paper.

We walked to the front of the bus and asked the driver what was going on. He seemed surprised to see us and gave us the dead-eye stare. "Where are we? When are we going back to town?" I asked. "*Non ritorno,*" he said. "*Sciopero! Non va!*"

I told him I thought it was just the trains on strike not the buses. "No—*tutti scoperio. Vai, Vai,*" he replied, and ordered us off the bus.

Across from the bus were ten to twelve camper caravan vehicles parked in a semi-circle where an encampment of French Gypsies was setting up a traveling circus. It looked like something out of David Lynch's *Elephant Man*, but not all sepia-toned and backlit. Instead of lions and tigers and bears, they had pigs and sheep and chickens. It was a low-budget version of Siegfried and Roy—a barnyard circus

We managed to find the ringleader, or ringmaster rather, who spoke Italian, and I explained our situation. He said one of his people was driving into town and we could ride along. We followed him to a little three-wheeled vehicle, the sort that pass as trucks in Italy, and he told us to wait there. While we waited I examined the miniature truck, which was really nothing more than a large Tonka toy consisting of a tiny seating compartment up front and a small open cargo area in the back. It was basically a gas-powered wheelbarrow.

A few moments later the ringleader returned with a dwarf holding a chicken.

The dwarf, who appeared to be not more than three feet tall, was to be our driver. And the wheelbarrow was to be our transportation. *Oh well,* I thought, *at least he was small, better than the bearded lady.* After we all crammed into the impossibly small seat and packed in as tight as *acciugi* (sardines)—the ringleader handed the dwarf the chicken. This disturbed me and I asked why the chicken couldn't ride in back in a crate or something, but it turns out this was no ordinary chicken—it was the star of the circus—and we're told that it plays piano (albeit a small one) and walks a tightrope. So I guess the chicken had some clause in its contract that said it gets to travel first class at all times and probably no brown M&M's in the dressing room as well.

Oh yeah, and the chicken's name is—I kid you not—Claude. So it's me, Claudia, Claude, and the dwarf, off to see the wizard. I made Claudia hold the chicken since I figured she might have more experience with this sort of thing being from Shanghai and all, but she was not happy about it.

After a few false starts the sputtering cart pulled out to the road and hit our top cruising speed of twelve miles an hour. As we chugged along I discovered our oompa loompa spoke some English and he told me that he was taking Claude, the star chicken, to see the vet in town because he was sick. I immediately freaked out and thought *holy shit, a sick chicken! — SARS! Avian Flu!* And I tried not to breathe for the next thirty minutes.

When we arrived in town Claudia and I were covered in pinfeathers. I felt like I need to be de-loused. I tried to make a joke to Claudia about how the whole experience was *completely plucked* but it was impossible to translate and really not that funny. Besides it seemed that Claudia had momentarily lost her sense of humor after being pecked at for the entire trip. I couldn't decide what was worse, the constant pecking of Claude, or the driver draping his stumpy paw on my knee as he shifted gears.

Later that evening when my host family Marco and Elizabetta asked me how Florence was, I told them *"Sciopero, non vado."* They both nodded and with weary looks on their faces said—*"Ah, si, sciopero."*

⌒⌒

Marcy Gordon operates a marketing and publicity consulting firm, Bocca della Verita, which provides marketing services to travel guidebook publishers. She is a contributing editor to the new Authentic Italy series published by the Touring Club of Italy.

18

FRANCESCA DE STEFANO

PARADISO

In a serene place, a scream doesn't fit—
or does it?

I HAVE JUST STEPPED FROM THE SHOWER WHEN I FIRST HEAR a voice that seems loud for its surroundings. Workers in the pocket piazza under my hotel-room windows calling out to each other, I'm sure. I'd seen some men down there the day before, hammering on cobblestones.

But the voice, words slurred and fast, mostly incomprehensible, swells and I begin to understand a few words: *putain,* whore, *cattivo*, bad. I grab a towel and grip it in one fist in front, then hair dripping, hurry to the window. From here, the voice is louder; it is still difficult to make out individual words. All I can see is a wedge of the deserted piazza, unshadowed in the bright afternoon sun.

I recognize *putain* once again. Someone is very angry. In such a setting, who could be making this ugly scene? And why was no one stopping him?

My husband, Carlo, and I are staying in Castello de Gargonza, a tiny walled town curled like a snail around its ancient crenelated tower. This entire egg-shaped hamlet, set in lush woods near the border between Tuscany and Umbria, has been transformed into a hotel.

Visitors enter through Dante's Gate, leaving their cars secreted in a wooded parking lot. Dante's sojourn here in 1302, after he was expelled from Florence for political activities unattractive to the Florentines, is the hamlet's claim to historical significance.

Otherwise, generations lived a simple, feudal life here. Though the aristocratic families that "owned" Gargonza changed a few times over the centuries, the townspeople always held the rights to the forest, to the hunting for game and foraging for mushrooms and grazing stock that made subsistence endurable. They must have been people of independent spirit, since the town apparently made its own laws and elected its own leaders.

After World War II, the flight to the cities emptied this village as it did others all over Europe. By 1964, there were only 19 residents left, down from 300, and by 1970, only 4. There are photographs at Gargonza of the village then, crumbling heaps of pale stone, roofs beginning to cave in. Within a short time, it could easily have disappeared into the trees.

Instead, Count Roberto Guicciardini, whose family has controlled the village since the eighteenth century, refused to allow his beloved Gargonza to disappear. In the 1970s, he spearheaded a restoration. Not only would he aspire to save the village by making it into a hotel, he would try to appeal to a certain type of tourist, one who would forego luxury, and be compelled by history. In addition, he set out to attract musicians to play at Gargonza, and music lovers, to listen. Now there are castle-hotels all over Italy from the Dolomites to Sicily. But this was one of the first.

The Count insisted that the restorers choose authenticity over extravagance, convenience, or modernity. So, while there are electricity and modern plumbing at Gargonza, our bathroom is small and inconvenient. There is heat, but not air conditioning. All the accommodations have low, beamed ceilings and small, wood-framed windows. Fireplaces crackle, warming the air on chilly nights, but the furniture is simple, like what might be found in a farmhouse.

I am so moved to be here with this capable bride, poised at the beginning of her life, I kiss her on both cheeks and wish her *"Auguri,"* luck.

All of the hotel rooms, which are actually apartments and houses of various sizes, have been named for their former inhabitants. I have fallen in love with the brochure descriptions of the Castello's last inhabitants, such as the room called Celso Piattelli, after the man who "experienced the rebirth of Gargonza. He took care of the wood, hunting, and all the estate's activities." Or Lucia, "for the weaver who transformed the wool produced here into fabric." Our tiny apartment is named Tullio, for Tullio Bartolomei, a watchman who "also performed administrative duties." I think about Tullio, since I'm living in his home and it occurs to me that it's good he had some administrative duties to keep him busy when he wasn't watching for intruders.

There are no shops at Gargonza; there is no pizza by the slice or otherwise; there is no tourist booty to escape with except the wine and olive oil produced here. Outside the walls, a restaurant in an old stone outbuilding and a pool with a storybook view of the tower allow guests to spend as much time here as they wish, but without interfering with the medieval verisimilitude of the Castello.

Of course, this is no longer a real home for anyone. But it's easy to understand the pragmatic, practical Tuscan (think of all those soups made from stale bread and vegetables!) pact the Count made: his beloved Gargonza could disappear, or it could become what it is—a place where people come and stay and play music in the olive press, where Mass is celebrated in the tiny church every Sunday, attended by people from local villages (three of the Count's own grandchildren were baptized here). It is a place that provides jobs to people who live nearby, like the waiter from Cortona who told us he'd worked at a restaurant in North Beach in our own San Francisco last winter, a job obtained for him by the now-famous Cortonese, Frances Mayes.

The Count is in his eighties and lives a couple of hours away in Florence, but rumors are always swirling that he has just made a visit or will be making one soon.

"You just missed him," one of the young women who run the place tells us when we stop by the office. There are usually two or three of these young women, by the look of them fresh from university, checking in guests or giving directions. They all seem capable of pegging the country of origin of each newcomer by the opening, "*Buon giorno,*" and greeting them in the appropriate language.

I note that they speak English with small mistakes in tense or the endings of words, the kinds of mistakes I am forever wincing at when I realize I've made them in Italian. They are all quite polite and helpful, even my least favorite, who is rather stiff and proper for an Italian. She is not pretty but has fine eyes, large and light blue, and dark blond hair. When I ask her how she knew to speak English to me, she says, "Did you wish us to speak with you in Italian, Signora?"

We are enraptured by Castello de Gargonza, rambling among its bisque-colored stone buildings and narrow passages. The place is so small, yet ideally designed. One grassy garden is lush with lemon trees and a view of the rolling green Valdichiana below; a peek through the doorway into another walled garden reveals neat rows of vegetables. My favorite thing about the Castello is the pine grove: a patch of forest encroaching inside the castle walls. We savor a moment's refuge from the sun, strolling through this miniature forest of tall pines.

The spot is so romantic, it's not surprising that couples marry here. One morning, taking a stroll after breakfast, laid out lavishly each day in the olive press, I spot a group of several young women decorating the little Romanesque church with ribbons and flowers. One crouches to steady a stepladder for her slight friend, who balances on the ladder in a short dress. The decorator is standing on tiptoe in pale flat shoes, twisting creamy tulle ribbon above double wooden doors.

When I ask, *"Dov'e la sposa?* Where is the bride?" the miniskirt-clad girl steps delicately down the couple of steps from her perch.

"Eccomi," Here I am, she says, and stands before me. She has wavy brown hair, a heart-shaped face, and a lovely smile.

I am so moved to be here with this capable bride, poised at the beginning of her life, I kiss her on both cheeks and wish her *"Auguri,"* luck, and, *"Una vita lunga e felice."* A long and happy life. She transfers a length of the ribbon from her hands to mine, and I amble off with a light heart. I have that scrap of ribbon still.

Later, we hear beeping horns and cheering and hurry to the gate to watch a big touring car drive partway round the egg-shaped village, down the driveway to the main road and back again only to repeat the circuit.

"Carlo, hurry. Come here and listen to this," I call, when I hear my husband push open the door and climb the stone steps inside our little apartment. He joins me at the window and stands silent, listening. This is not a marital spat; someone is enraged here.

"Who could it be?" I ask him. "Who is he, and why is he yelling like that?"

"I don't know. I could hear him as soon as I came back inside the walls." He stands still, listening again. There is no relief from the sound.

"If you want to go to Monteriggioni today," he reminds me, and I know he wants to go, to flee that voice, "we really need to leave now."

"We have to tell somebody," I say, torn. "What if he's hurting someone?"

"Who? Listen. You can't hear anyone else."

I listen. It's true. "You're right, but I'll feel better if we stop by the office on the way out and tell one of the girls. The hotel should deal with this."

The voice never ceases as we walk over to the office. I feel a headache developing at the base of my neck. Outside, the voice seems even louder. I turn to look in every direction, wondering why people aren't running out of their rooms to stop this sound. But when we reach the office door, the sign is clear from several yards away. *Chiuso,* closed. Of course—by now it's siesta; no one will be available for hours.

The winding drive to Monteriggioni—a Tuscan hill town notable for picturesque walls and eight intact towers which once strengthened them against attack—is peaceful. We wander the town in the hot sun, eat dinner in the garden of a restaurant built into the walls, and the raving voice seems distant and fantastic. There must have been some mistake, or I have misunderstood, perhaps one of those cultural things.

In the darkness, we leave the car and enter the Castello through Dante's gate. Floodlights on the tower cast shadows on the cobblestone piazza and its octagonal fountain. The silence, benign this morning, is eerie tonight. No longer innocent, now it is the absence of the sound of that screaming voice.

Later, my husband tells me that, while I was brushing my

teeth, he found a lizard under my pillow, one of the harmless tiny green variety. He knew that normally I would have laughed, but then meticulously checked the bed to be sure it hadn't left any compatriots behind. Reading my mood, he carefully picked up our visitor and placing it outside, checked the bed carefully himself, not breathing a word to me.

My husband falls into an easy sleep, as he always does. And, as is often true, I am maddened by the way he can do this in nearly any situation. I sleep fitfully; when I open my eyes several times during the night, the low-beamed ceiling, so close to my face, seems oppressive.

In the morning I wake early, bundling my things into suitcases, half sorry, half relieved that we are scheduled to leave. I offer to pay the bill while my husband packs the car. Eager for an explanation and expecting an apology, I am disappointed to see that the blond girl, the one I find least *simpatica*, is on duty. She hands me an itemized bill and I put it aside while I think of how to begin.

"There was a man yesterday," I say. "He was screaming and swearing. For a long time. *Multo forte,*" *Very loud*, I add. I want to be sure she understands.

She regards me calmly, pale eyes unblinking. "Oh yes, signora," she says, then slowly, each word separated by a pause, as if she too wants to be sure I understand, "That is a mad person."

"A mad person," I parrot stupidly.

"That man comes here, the priest brings him," she replies, still impassive. "Some of the times this happens. Not usually."

"Well, I just wanted to be sure," I say in a weak voice, "that no one was in danger."

"Oh, no, no. You know," she continues, confiding, "the authorities would like to put him in an institution." And she shakes her head in bewilderment over the imponderable cruelty of these heartless "authorities."

"How terrible," I say, mirroring her shaking head, giving the bill a cursory check, and signing before handing over the credit card slip. "Well, thank you for explaining. Goodbye."

"*Arrivederci.* Please come back, signora. I hope we will see you again."

We are all the way down the hill, past Monte San Savino and almost to the entrance to the *autostrada* before the enchantment begins to wear off, and I ask myself: Is the priest *pazzo*, crazy, himself, bringing a lunatic to conduct an ear-splitting fit at a hotel? And are he and the girl both out of their respective minds, to think it would be a tragedy to send an insane person to an insane institution?

I decide that this could never happen in the United States and, if it did, the hotel guests would be demanding their money back and deserting the place in an exodus. Yet, I have to admit, I am more charmed than outraged, more beguiled than affronted. I wonder if the Count knows, and decide that he probably does. If I had the opportunity to ask him, I think he would say that all of them, the mad person and the blond and the priest, are part of the real life he meant to nurture at Gargonza.

Francesca De Stefano, who lives in San Francisco with her husband and son, is writing a book of travel essays set in Italy. She credits her love of travel to one of her first childhood memories, standing at the dock in New York, holding one end of some streamers, her grandparents holding the other, as their boat left the dock for a visit home to Italy.

19

ANNE CALCAGNO

KICKED INTO THE MEDITERRANEAN

The world of things Italian is both international and very very local.

MY SISTER AND I LEFT HOME IN ITALY IN THE 1980S TO ATTEND universities in the U.S., freed of our parents. We didn't give them much more than cursory thought until, at our separate locations, we received the same bizarre packet of photos. At the center of each photo was a fissured gray storeroom barricaded by a splintered slab of wood. In front of this blight came a picture of mom smiling, then dad smiling, then the two of them smiling. The telltale caption read: "Our new home on the sea!" My sister and I were on the phone instantly, in clear agreement that their mental proclivities were in rapid decline, brought on by our cruel abandon.

Of course, we were wrong. I soon learned that when you give your heart to Sicily, as they had done, you choose passion over logic. Yet how few of Sicily's fans are Americans, despite the fact that the largest portion of

Italian-Americans descends from Italy's poor south and poorer Sicily. *Most* tourists to Italy never reach Sicily. It remains the soccer ball Italy boots into the deep blue sea. Gorgeous triangle, lemon-laden. Invaded, restored, ignored, plundered. Left repeatedly to rot, socially, economically, and politically. Ripe territory for neorealist filmmakers. For the great writers such as Giovanni di Lampedusa, Dacia Maraini, Giovanni Verga, Elio Vittorini. Splashed by a Mediterranean so ultramarine it hurts the eye. Yet always and again desperate for water. For jobs. For Mt. Etna to keep her temper at bay. For the west coast to contain its Mafia.

In truth, it wasn't mainland Sicily that unlocked my parents' "storeroom of dreams." They'd headed west of Sicily's west coast—leaving behind the gold Greek ampitheater of Segesta, the high medieval town of Erice, Trapani's wide salt flats and bustling port—to board a ferry to the Egadi Islands: Favignana, Levanzo, and Marettimo, three rocky shores as unfrequented as they are distant.

Though such isolation was, for centuries, untrue.

Human habitation on these lands goes back 11,000 years. Some say farther. In Levanzo's Grotta del Genovese paleolithic graffiti depict human figures and, most importantly, tuna, long the mainstay of these islands.

Around the eighth century B.C. the Phoenicians used Favignana as a port of call named Katria. The Romans would rename her Aegusa, and brought their Punic Wars upon her. Legend has it that Favignana's most gorgeous *super*-turquoise bay was once red with the blood of defeated Carthaginians. Hence today's anachronistic name: Cala Rossa (Red Bay). Islanders claim that Favignana shipwrecked Odysseus and offered him troublesome Calypso. Saracens built lookout towers on Favignana and Marettimo. Normans, corsairs, pirates, Spaniards, Bourbons left inscriptions and hideouts carved deep into the islands' sandstone.

Why? Location, location, location. Kicked into the middle of the Mediterranean, nothing interrupts the view. What better lookout posts? Plus, every single one of the eight winds of the windrose (Tramontana, Grecale, Levante, Libeccio, Ostro, Scirocco, Ponente, Maestrale) beats upon these shores. Varied and shifting, the preponderance of differing winds makes these

---

I will always point my way south, ready for the long plane ride, the cab, then the hydrofoil, into the searing North African heat, where nothing is more important than every single day.

---

islands perfect rest stops for seafarers. Today, tourists purchase guidebooks advising which beaches match the day's wind direction. It's one way, even during a short stay, that you cannot but explore the islands' different beaches. The advantages offered by such complex challenging wind conditions were not lost on the 2005 America's Cup. Dramatic race trials were held off Trapani in October. A children's sailing school has sprung up on Favignana, along with scuba diving, fishing excursions with pasta lunches, and an increasing number of art shops and local events.

Yet the essential simplicity of these islands—rocky sunbeaten land skimming pristine waters casually rich with fish—has changed little in the twenty years since my parents began restoring their fisherman's storage area, one in a string of sweet, cramped, white-washed storerooms to become tiny homes facing the indigo sea. The Egadis pause in time, a brilliant caesura. I have traveled back to Italy, north and center, to cities and countryside, many, many times. And I cannot cite such a time-freeze about much of modern Italy. For the Egadis' lack of acceleration, I will always point my way south, ready for the long plane ride, the cab, then the hydrofoil, into the searing North African heat, where nothing is more important than every single day.

Daily life used to be at the center of Italian existence. Now who has the time?

As little girls growing up in Milan, we were tacked onto Mom's daily routine to the baker, fruit monger, butcher, deli vendor, milkman, tobacconist (for stamps, salt, matches), and wine seller. Each store was an encounter, a visit to familiar faces, neighbors and merchants alike, some of whom we invented stories about, fed by local gossip or our own eager imaginations. The daily journey infuriated my young mother eager to be about her life which she didn't much posit in grocery shopping. But these days, my sister, mom, and I head together into Favignana's small old center, over the large shiny gray paving stones, smelling bread and fish and espresso and ice cream. If the Thursday and Saturday *mercatini* (little markets) aren't setting up until *domani*, we visit the farmer for fresh ricotta, then we cover the stores one by one, religiously; we buy piping hot rolls from the vast family of redheads; capers, watermelon, prickly pears, tomatoes, lemons from the tiny widow who always clenches my mom's hand at length in affectionate greeting. Always, you can choose *bottarga* (dried tuna eggs, a specialty, truffle-like, grated onto pasta) or carefully packed local tuna. Tuna that once was the islands' greatest wealth.

Large schools of *Thunnus Thynnus* have for thousands of years pressed through the Egadi on their run from the Atlantic to mate in the Mediterranean's warmer waters. Every May, the *mattanza* is still conducted, a gruesome, if theatrical, trapping and harpooning of a dense rush of enormous tuna. In years past a particular delicacy famous throughout Italy, this tuna no longer supports an active economy but there's still plenty of it to savor, along with squid, urchin, octopus, and any other catch of the day.

. In Favignana, they stuff ice cream into sweet rolls for breakfast. Or, in the evening, you can join long rows of ice-cream eaters planted like theatergoers in plastic chairs along the narrow street, watching the town *passegiata*. And, of course, the tourists, bearing tattoos and skimpy new fashions. Rare among them any Americans.

My parents, now retired and in their seventies, are less enamored by the daily shopping rigamarole, which *is* a labor of love. But they can't (though they could) seem to leave. Yes, habit kills fascination. And I don't live here. Yet every time I return, I am mostly a young girl about the business of her day, buying the basics for those I love. I retrieve my past; here very present. I get something utterly simple, but rarely available—each fig, squid, slice of warm *focaccia* (salty flatbread that tastes in Sicily like nowhere else) born to be relinquished just on this day, the day I'm living. I enter a journey much bigger than mine, conscious of this swirling earth, precious because temporary, newborn, so intensely delicious.

Favignana is the largest and most habitable of the Egadis, and so remains the one with most stories. The Italian painter, Salvatore Fiume, painted her as *La Farfalla Sul Mare* (Butterfly on the Sea) noting her distinctive shape—a narrow waistline is topped by a mountain from which two wide spreads of dry land unfold—and the name has stuck. Sicily's more famous and glamour-craving Aeolian Islands, north and east of the Egadis, have volcanic origins. But the Egadis originate in glaciated deposits, residues that built layer upon layer of *tufo* (sandstone) of superior quality. For centuries the Egusei, as the islanders are named, quarried *tufo*, backbreaking work chiseling large square blocks with picks. This source of construction material was the second principal economy of the island until the advent of reinforced concrete, post-World War II. Today, you can take the local sandstone home in the form of local outdoor sculptures.

One leaves town—bicycles a preferred method of transport—past waist-high walls of craggy sandstone, their interstices as narrow as mosaic work. I love to stop to look *down* these walls at the *tufo* houses. Many are built ten, fifteen meters below street level, some out of abandoned *tufo* quarries, but all chosen as viable locations because tunneling into the sandstone offers coolness and shade. Caper bushes spill down the walls to where chickens scrabble, cats stretch, and grape arbors amble crookedly along. Stairways are famous here, down to homes, up to rooftop terraces, up and down to the fresh cold sapphire sea. They curve around the craggy coasts that sport secret caves everywhere, shade spots, lunch spots. These are islands carved by sea and man.

Where now the limited and frail principal economy is tourism. Not that I'm inviting.

~ↄ

Anne Calcagno has written travel pieces for The New York Times *and the* Chicago Tribune, *and is the editor of* Travelers' Tales Italy.

20

DEBORAH J. SMITH

IF I WERE POPE

Don't miss this stairway to heaven.

MY SECOND TIME IN ROME, I DIDN'T WANT TO MISS CLIMB-ing the Dome of Saint Peter's. Last trip, the tempera-ture was 104 degrees—too hot to go up in an enclosed space. But now it was early spring, and I was lined up with my five euros and my digital camera, ready to hop on the elevator and walk out into the eerie mag-nificence of Michelangelo's masterpiece.

The elevator drops you at the first stop: a walkway around the interior cupola of the basilica. An iron grid protects the tourists above from falling down to the tour-ists below, but you still get a good look—or some good snapshots—of the church interior. Then it's upward to all those stairs.

Along the way heavenward, Saint Peter's is designed with small windows and angular air spaces that give a keyhole view of the city. At times, ledges appear so you can sit, look out, and wonder if the dome is moving or it's your own vertigo from too many close turns round and round the steps. As you climb, the walkway and the walls narrow. It is possible, just before the end, to stand on a step, look forward and see that the dome wall is now 45 degrees from vertical. And yes, it is getting very, very close inside.

Steps supporting a single person access the last part of the climb. There are no handrails; visitors must hold a thick rope suspended from the top. Inscribed on marble as you reach the end of the stairs is *"Giro Della Prima Ringhiera Esterna."* Translated from the Italian, it is "Turn of the First External Railing." I was translating very loosely and romantically; I thought it meant "Entering the First Ring of Eternity." If eternity is skyward, this surely looks like the beginning of the ascent.

The narrow walkway now slopes toward the outer railing where most tourists congregate—it's also possible to walk around the top of the dome through the inner columns. Great panoramic shots of Saint Peter's Square are taken here: you can see the entirety of the Vatican Gardens, outward to the Imperial Forum itself, and over the city of Rome to seemingly forever. The views from the top of St. Peter's Basilica are spectacular.

Walking around to see each bit of the view, I found myself wondering if the Pope has ever seen the city from these heights. After all, the popes live here. Do they ever come up to the dome to pray, or watch the tiny specks of people drifting across the square below? Or are popes just too busy to see the beauty right above their heads? And he's a travelin' man, there may not be much free time in his schedule. But...

I know what I'd do if I were Pope. For a single night—maybe on my birthday—I'd stop leading my flock to the eternal Grace of God. The heads of state could visit elsewhere and the encyclicals could lie untouched for an evening. Don't boil water for the pasta until I return.

If I were Pope, I'd collar a few trusted Swiss Guards, my best friends, and the master keys to the dome. I'd escape up the elevator with a flashlight in the darkest hour before dawn and walk quietly onto the first ring of eternity.

There, in the darkness, I'd appreciate how beautiful it is at this moment. I'd walk around and marvel at the magnificence of the Eternal City at night, sparkling like diamonds on velvet.

If I were Pope, I'd sit there until the sun rose and I could see the whole vista in daylight, too. Then, before the tourists came, we'd all go back to the Vatican apartments for cappuccino and *cornettos* and the rest of the day's schedule. At the next Mass, I'd thank God for making this view as far as the eye can see so gorgeous and giving me, as Pope, a real chance to enjoy it.

Maybe the Pope does get up to the bottom of eternity…I don't know for sure. Ever since I've been up to the top, and stopped halfway down to see the towering statues of the Apostles that gaze out on the Square, my view of Saint Peter's has been forever changed. Now I watch for the small black ring appearing just above the main expanse of the dome, and I smile—because that's a line of tourists looking out over the city.

There is no doubt about it. St. Peter's Basilica is the most magnificent church on earth, from the top down or the bottom up. I'd make the time to find this out—especially if I were Pope.

Deborah J. Smith is a faculty member with Empire State College's International Program in Lebanon, where she teaches the courses "Stories of Food and Culture" and "Around the World: Travel Writing." She has written about travel, food, and faith for various publications including Tastes of Italia *magazine, the* Rome Italy Tourist Portal, *the* Berkshire Women's Times, *and Traveler's Tales anthologies. Smith is a native of Troy, New York, and her work is frequently broadcast on Northeast Public Radio.*

21

DAVID DARLINGTON

WINE FIASCOS

In Italy, a "fiasco" might be a bottle of Chianti
—or it might not.

FOR THE SEMI-KNOWLEDGEABLE WINE BUFF, TRAVEL IN EUROPE
can be a dream—or it can be an adult version of pin-the-
tail-on-the-donkey. Success depends, as in most areas of
travel, on how adventurous you are, how well you know
the language, and how much guff you're willing to give
(and take from) people who can hardly understand you
to start with.

On a recent trip to Italy, my experience bore a decided resemblance to the parlor embarrassments of youth:
don a blindfold, spin around, and stick your companions
with something that only a mule would accept.

The game wasn't made any easier by the local rules.
Italy produces and sells more wine than almost any other
country on earth—a circumstance heralding good news
and bad. On the up side, wine is everywhere; however, as
the venerable Hugh Johnson writes in *The World Atlas of
Wine*, "Italy has a serious drawback: an impossible confusion of names. Because wine is omnipresent, so much a

part of everyday life, made by so many proud and independent people, every conceivable sort of name is pressed into use to mark originality." Factor in the national characteristic of go-with-the-flow insouciance (not to say passivity or indifference) and you can find yourself groping for an oenological donkey as big as a brontosaurus.

My first fiasco occurred near the town of Voghera, on the border between Lombardy and Piedmont, southwest of Milan—excellent wine country, as it happens. By way of a disclaimer, let me note that I was traveling with a group of American bicyclists—people not especially noted for their gourmet tastes. (A wine buff doesn't know the meaning of depression until he asks a table of a dozen people, "Who wants wine?" and nobody raises a hand.)

On this particular evening, four of us had gotten separated from the main group, so an opportunity suddenly loomed to eat something other than pizza for dinner. We made our way to the nearest town and found the central square, where a clutch of nattily attired students informed us that it was a holiday and everything was closed. Except, that is, for a pizzeria.

The joint was jumping when we arrived, which we took to bode well (even if it was the only open place in town). There were lots of wine bottles on the walls, but Italian Wine Problem #2 is that relatively few restaurants offer anything other than general categories on their wine lists. The most important things to know are years and producers, but a typical list will say only: "Barbera—Dolcetto—Valpolicella," etc.

In this simple small-town eatery, most of the names were so obscure that even my pocket wine encyclopedia failed to include them. I did recognize a word in one of the names, however: Sangiovese, the principal grape of Chianti. I pointed it out to the waiter and sat back, anticipating a satisfying encounter with an unknown—but undoubtedly delicious—local wine.

American yuppies abroad might be surprised to learn how finicky Italians aren't about wine. For example, seldom is seen such foolishness as displaying a label before pulling a cork or offering a taste to the person who ordered. Our waiter had uncorked the bottle before it reached our table, where he banged it down and vanished without so much as a "*Va bene?*"

Unfortunately, I could already see through the backlit glass that *bene* it wasn't. There was another word in the name that I'd overlooked: "Rosato." As I could now clearly see, in this stronghold of solid red wine, I'd ordered a rosé.

Oh well—live and learn. On to the Alps and the town of Aosta. In the morning I climbed a mountain on my bicycle, then spent the late afternoon strolling around the city, an ancient Roman colony. On a side street near the glacier-fed Dora Baltea River, I watched a car full of correspondents from *La Gazzetta dello Sport* pull up and pile into a trattoria. Needless to say, these veteran cycling journalists didn't share my companions' aversion to the grape.

On the way back to my hotel, I stumbled on a beguiling little restaurant in an alley. Decorated with a colorful painting of a funny-looking bird, it was called Pam Pam—Trattoria degli Artiste. I asked a lady in the store next door if the place was good, and she said that it was. So I returned that evening with three friends: one American, one French, one Italian.

In the entryway were several photographs of the tanned, mustachioed, curly-haired proprietor with tanned, mustachioed, curly-haired Italian pop stars. A cornucopia of glistening antipasti graced a side table; another inviting collection of wine bottles adorned the wall. Nevertheless, the list still showed nothing but types.

Determined to get a good wine this time, I decided to ask the owner for help. In his stead, a sommelier appeared: lean, narrow-eyed, and unsmiling, the man seemed to regard me with suspicion. I asked the vintage of the Chianti Classico; he answered 1995, which at the time seemed a bit young. The other choices—Barbera, Bardolino, et al.—though undoubtedly decent, didn't pique my interest. There was, however, an Amarone, a red wine from the Veneto that I'd heard described as big and rich. The steward said it was a '91.

This time he poured me a taste, though in retrospect I'm not sure why. I took a sniff and wrinkled my face. The wine smelled old or oxidized or something, the way it would if it had been stored over a stove. I offered the glass to my Italian companion, who simply said: "So strong!" The sommelier himself took a whiff, glanced at me from the corner of his eye, and muttered, "*Particolare.*"

Reluctant to cause a ruckus, I shrugged and accepted the wine. Then, true to emerging form, I found out what I'd ordered by examining the label in closer detail. The wine was 16 percent alcohol—a late-harvest level of strength, arrived at by drying grapes in the sun after harvest. According to a hangtag on the bottle, this technique had resulted in an "excellent dessert wine." *Particolare*, indeed.

By the last night of the trip, I was ready to quit being creative. Chastened by my own spirit of enterprise, I suggested that we eat at a pizzeria and ordered a trusty Barbera as soon as we sat down; I didn't even ask the year.

It turned out to be a 1994 Barbera del Monferrato. I fondled the brown-tinted bottle warmly, sanguine in my abandonment of initiative, ready to relax with a regular wine, laid-back as the Italians themselves who simply order "*Rosso.*" Until, that is, I poured it into my glass and it started fizzing.

As a home winemaker, I've seen that fizz before. To me it indicated instability: excess yeast, the dreaded brettanomyces, incomplete malolactic fermentation—bacteria continuing to do something in the bottle that they're supposed to have quit doing. Fizz is intentional in sparkling wine, where yeast and sugar are added to induce it, but red wine is supposed to keep still.

I poured more of it into my glass, hoping that the bubbles would disappear as they sometimes will when exposed to air. No luck. Perhaps influenced by the visual effect, I was now sure that the wine tasted yeasty. Trying to play things safe and conservative, I'd gotten a defective bottle. If only to appease myself for the disappointments of the trip, I called the young waitress over.

"*Una problema*," I said as pleasantly as possible. Then, pointing to the bottle, "*Frizzante*." The girl's smile disappeared, as did she. In her place appeared a swarthy sergeant-at-arms, a man who obviously wasn't inclined to take any crap from tourists. I noticed over my shoulder that several other waiters had assembled, and every diner in the room was looking at my table.

The martinet frowned at the glass, then at me. He said, in effect: "It's normal. Shut up and eat." Then he walked away.

At that point I determined not to pay. But then, as if from on high, another waiter appeared. He asked what was the matter, and when I repeated the F word, he studied the glass for a moment. Then he too departed, but he returned a moment later with another bottle, identical to the first except for two things: The new one was a '95, not a '94; and the label on the fizzy one contained an extra word that I, er, hadn't noticed. The word was *vivace*, meaning "lively."

In any case, the angelic peacemaker gave us the '95, which turned out to be utterly delicious. My companions were more impressed that I'd identified "liveliness" than annoyed that I'd missed it on the label (not that it would have mattered, I rush to reiterate, since they open it as soon as you order it anyway). The room's other patrons returned to their meals, and for the first time on the trip the wine finally did its proper job, imbuing the table with a great glow and a buoyant, jocular sense of well-being. Celebrating our averting of an international incident, we left the waitress a tip so huge that she came running after us, trying to return it. As we were leaving, the Good Waiter made a point of shaking my hand.

When I got back to the hotel, I found my pocket guide and looked up Barbera del Monferrato. It was described as "pleasant and slightly fizzy."

For wine buffs, it seems, a little knowledge is a dangerous thing.

༄

David Darlington is the author of Area 51: The Dreamland Chronicles, The Mojave: A Portrait of the Definitive American Desert, Angels' Visits: An Inquiry into the Mystery of Zinfandel, *and* Zin: The History and Mystery of Zinfandel.

22

MARAEL JOHNSON

PSALM JOURNEY

The ancient concept of sanctuary acquires new meaning.

"ARE YOU CATOLICA?" ASKED SISTER MARCELLINA.

Oh God, what was I this week? Unitarian, Hindu, Jewish, Born-Again, something New Age? My religion usually depends on what holiday I do or do not want to celebrate, or the biases and proclivities of the country or people I happen to be visiting. (Recently I became an instant convert to the Pentecostal sect of the mechanic who was performing a tricky smog inspection on my emissions-tampered race car.)

This was an easy call—I was living in a convent in Assisi, Christmas was a long way off—and the demonic speedster back in California was legal for another two years. Yeah, sure, I was Catholic.

"It doesn't matter," she said, "but I wonder because you're following in the footsteps of Saint Francis."

St. Francis? The bird- and animal-lover, right? Wonderful! I adore animals—even the ones I eat. On the other hand, those vows to poverty, obedience, and chastity were my three most hated virtues.

The sisters had me wrong (or so I thought). I hadn't come to their convent to contemplate the life of Saint Francis—my presence was purely an accident. A few weeks earlier I'd been brutally attacked by a drug-crazy teenager (also a bird- and animal-lover)—a puny surfer who had punched me in the jaw, banged me against my own wooden walls and well-worn antiques, and then nearly strangled me to death. It was a pathetic scene. I had cowered defenseless, hysterical, shaking, sobbing—like a beaten animal, a bird without flight, like the battered woman I had been in what had seemed like a thousand incarnations ago. What was it he'd said before he left (appeased by $200 cash and his newly discovered "power")? "You've been beaten before." Yes, yes, I remember nodding, like some cheap bobbing-head souvenir. His arrogant shrug cocked me a line: "If you've been beaten 2000 times, what's 2001?"

It was the one that sent me to the convent.

I'd only come for two days—a brief respite from visiting friends in France where I'd given what was left of myself away, sobbing into the *café au lait* each morning. I'd actually been headed to an ashram about thirty miles from Assisi. My plan had been to dive into meditation (and ever deeper into my bare-handed-castration and hired-hitman fantasies) while cooking my nightmares away inside cauldrons of vegetarian stew. It didn't work out. By the time I'd found the ashram—a three-train, one-bus, and thumb-out ride from Florence—the place had been shut down by the Italian government. I'd been pointed to the convent where, for some inexplicable reason, every two days I asked to stay two days longer. I'd been there for weeks.

The convent was home to the Swedish Sisters of something-or-other, though none of the sisters were Swedish but Italian,

Ethiopian, Pakistani, and such. They wore gray habits with a pe-culiar type of headpiece, fastened by a clamplike device which made them all look as though they'd had frontal lobotomies. Two of the older sisters were suitably severe and unsmiling.

> Each day—like some gumshoe detective in search of an unfaithful spouse—I tailed Saint Francis to one of his haunts.

My room was on the second floor with views of the rose garden, the Umbrian hills, the lowlands beyond. It was long and nar-row—blissfully austere—with a long, narrow single bed made up with stiff unsoiled white sheets and a weightless virgin-wool blanket. A cheap imitation of the magical cross that spoke to Saint Francis hung over my head, and a mass-produced print of our Swedish patron saint stared from the desk. Cappuccino was served each morning and Chianti was poured at night. Everyone was celibate, everyone was sane. I was locked in. Safe.

The rooms were polished, perfectly kept. No one dared touch the classic volumes in the library, nor the ebony piano in the drawing room. The dining tables were always set with linen, heavy silver, hand-painted china, and spotless water glasses. Two younger sisters would arrive at my room each morning with cleaning supplies, only to find I had already made my bed (with hospital corners), wiped out the sink and bidet, and hung the thin woven towels out to dry.

The sisters thought I was very strange. And, of course, they were right.

I was a fairly well-to-do homeless person. An escapee, a wom-an on the run. All of my belongings were contained within one cheap, made-in-China roll-aboard—a long black wool (nun's?) dress, two pair of blue jeans, a couple of t-shirts, my most unsexy underwear, a practical nightgown, sensible shoes, no makeup, and a blue cashmere turtleneck pullover. I wore the pullover every day, carefully folding the neck to hide the deep scarlet gashes left by my near-strangulation—even though they'd become invisible to every eye except my own after about forty-eight hours. Without that covering I could see my burnished scars reflected in every piece of ancient stained glass, in the mirror of a cupboard used to store old habits, in the dark reaches of my crystalline memories.

I had no idea what my mission was, nor the meaning of my longer and longer stay. Each day—like some gumshoe detective in search of an unfaithful spouse—I tailed Saint Francis to one of his haunts: the huge very unFrancislike basilica where his tomb posed for tourists' cameras; the monastery where he began the Franciscan order; the room where he baptized Sister Moon Clare; the garden where he plunged his flesh into the thorny roses; the chapel where the cross spoke to him; to the very spots where he was born, punished, revered, had preached, and died. I mused on Giotto's colorful scenes and Raphael's seductive angels, made sketches on a stupid souvenir notepad with Saint Francis's image embedded on every tissue-y leaf. I sucked oranges with a dreadlocked teenage girl in the middle of an olive grove, resisted the advances of that Pietro guy over at the parking garage with his easy access to an isolated toilet. I pressed my hands against the glass that housed Saint Francis's tunic—its fabric so thick, so textured, beautifully patched with a painstaking overlock stitch in some places—pocked with gaping holes and tattered edges in other spots.

Eventually the Swedish sisters told me, "Be out by Friday!"

A feast was approaching and they needed my room. It was time to leave anyway—I was out of money, my Visa card kept getting rejected, and my clothes were filthy and falling apart (I'd already had to darn the pullover several times). I needed to get back to work. I needed to go home.

Home. I suddenly realized that most of my anger and despair had dissipated during my stay in Assisi and my murky following in the pink-marbled footsteps of Saint Francis. And though I was hardly at the point where I loved my enemies, at least I didn't hate them. What had changed? I'd been living much like Francis and his followers—cloistered, adhering to poverty, obedience, and chastity. There was a time I'd viewed those vows as the most dire of punishments (just a few weeks earlier, in fact). Now they had metamorphosed into valuable survival tools—more useful than a top-of-the-line Swiss Army knife and a flask full of cognac. I had followed Francis into and out of his world, brazening some sort of internal mercenary training camp for beaten, flightless, and battered beasts.

Come Friday morning, I left my Swedish sisters and Assisi to catch a pre-dawn train—the first leg of my long journey home. Looking back at the walled city through the tricky morning mist, it was easy to imagine a solid figure clad in a raggedy, loosely belted tunic. I tugged at the neck of my darned pullover, feeling the stitching give way, and a gape of fresh air.

Marael Johnson, with roots in Russia and Motown, is a bonafide alumnus of Hollywood High and one of the few students in her graduating class who is still alive and has never been incarcerated. As a freelance writer and poet, she works and travels throughout the world. She has authored books for The National Geographic Society and Avalon Travel's Moon Handbooks, and has been an editor and contributor to dozens of travel guides. She is the recipient of a Lowell Thomas Award and a Publisher's Marketing Association award for best guidebook. A sun-hating, non-swimming avid reader, she makes her home in a Southern California beach town filled with deeply tanned shallow thinkers.

23

DOUG LANSKY

LAST TROUT IN VENICE

A gondola lesson on the Grand Canal.

I'M SITTING HERE IN MY WET UNDERWEAR ON THE SIDE OF the Grand Canal waiting for my clothes to dry. I have a burning blister on my thumb, algae stains coating my pants, and I just swallowed a mouthful of Venetian canal water, which I believe is melting the lining of my stomach. To top things off, I'm pretty sure some passing tourist caught my accidental plunge into the canal on tape and will soon be making thousands of dollars on *Italy's Funniest Home Videos* at my expense.

How I ended up in the Grand Canal should come as no surprise. I was taking gondola-driving lessons. Hardly a "must-do" in Venice. Most simply come for the romance: cozy strolls along the canals with the sound of distant bells, small waves gently lapping against ancient *palazzos,* and, of course, the enchanting footsteps of the 25 million tourists with white sneakers who annually trample this slowly sinking city of 75,000 residents.

Learning to drive a gondola on the Grand Canal is like learning to ride a bike on the Long Island Expressway. Whizzing up and down the canals are water buses, water taxis, private cruising boats, supply boats taking food and merchandise to the stores, plus all the other gondolas—over four hundred of them. There are no driving lanes on this busy aquatic road. You can drive on the left side or the right or straight down the middle if you please.

The only rule I saw observed is that the biggest boat has the right of way. Does this method work? Well, during my three days in Venice, there were three separate boating fatalities.

Fortunately the other boat drivers had guessed that an absolute moron was piloting this gondola, and they managed to get out of our way.

The way I figured, there's only one oar, they move slowly, what could be easier? As I learned from Lucca, a fortysomething gondolier I met who offered to show me the ropes, it would be much easier to learn to pilot an oil tanker through the Strait of Magellan.

There aren't any gondola-driving schools, as such. Most gondoliers learn their trade from their fathers or uncles and then inherit the boats from them. Lucca's father, however, was a Venetian glassblower, and Lucca was a dental hygienist. Eight years ago, he decided he wanted to spend less time fighting plaque and more time at peace with the outdoors, so he put down $20,000, bought a gondola, and taught himself how to drive it.

The world is quite familiar with the famous image of these thirty-seven-foot black canoes. What many may not know is how they actually move. The *remo*, or oar, rests in a wooden fork that protrudes from the rear right of the gondola. Unlike in a row boat, you don't lift the paddle out of the water to bring it back into position for the next stroke. Nor do you push off the bottom of the canal, as I once suspected. Instead, you push forward, then feather the *remo* back under the water. And unlike in a canoe, you can't start paddling on the other side to compensate for a turn. Everything has to be done from the fork.

After a short demonstration, Lucca held onto a pole on the side of the canal to keep the boat in place while I gave it a try. My first problem was that the oar kept popping out of the fork, and the waves, the tidal current, and the substantial weight of the *remo* made it hard to get it back in position. After I managed a few strokes, he let go and we were off.

Immediately, Lucca began issuing a seemingly impossible set of instructions. The first was "Use your legs," then "Get your whole body into the rowing motion." As I did this, the oar popped out of the fork and I struggled to put it back in, nearly falling overboard in the process. With no forward momentum, we began drifting out of control toward several boats. "Look forward," he said, oblivious to the fact that I couldn't get the *remo* back into the fork while looking forward, and simply looking forward wouldn't accomplish much except indicate which side of the gondola to jump from before we were rammed by a much larger boat.

Signe, who had come along for the ride, looked almost as nervous as I did, and I could see her plotting how to abandon ship without getting the camera wet.

Fortunately the other boat drivers had guessed that an absolute moron was piloting this gondola, and they managed to get out of our way. It probably helped that Lucca was standing at the front of the boat, making the "get the hell out of the way" signal.

Next Lucca wanted me to turn the boat around. He took the *remo* and demonstrated. It looked simple, and, surprisingly, it was.

However, this technique only applied to turning the boat to the left. Turning it to the right was near impossible. The only way I could make a 90-degree right turn was to turn the boat to the left 270 degrees.

About forty minutes into the lesson, my arms felt as if I had been doing forty minutes of push-ups. I didn't have enough strength left to shake hands. So Lucca took over, did some more demonstrations, and guided the boat back to the gondola station for a break. Back on land, Lucca taught me the time-honored tradition of how gondoliers discreetly urinate into the canal: you stand on the dock, hold a board in one hand, and lean it against a pole to form a little...well, teepee, and do your business under that.

I asked Lucca about the singing. After all, all gondoliers sing, don't they? "I don't sing," he said.

"But I thought you all had to at least do 'O Sole Mio.'"

"No," he said, "that's a myth. There are a handful of gondoliers who sing, but you almost always have to pay extra for a singer to come along."

"Customers pay a fortune for forty-five minutes in a gondola and don't get a singer included?" I asked, incredulous.

"No, that costs extra. Didn't I just tell you that?"

When I began to get some feeling back in my arms, we pushed out for the next lesson. With considerably more traffic and bigger waves, it looked twice as intimidating. After a few near spills, my oar slipped out of the fork and I finally lost complete balance and tumbled rather dramatically (twirling arms and all) into the drink, which, unfortunately, is what I inadvertently did as I came up for air. The water was murky brown, more biologically aggressive than anything in Iraq's arsenal, and tasted like month-old dishwater mixed with ammonia and a touch of diesel oil. I tried (unsuccessfully) to forget that Lucca and I had peed into this canal less than an hour ago.

Lucca couldn't stop laughing. Neither could Signe, who managed to capture the entire event on film. So did a water taxi full of videotaping tourists.

Just then something brushed my leg. I tried not to think what it could be, but my mind was already racing. A lone trout that had innocently mistaken the water for cappuccino? The dead body of a tourist weighted down by camera equipment?

I swam hurriedly to the edge of the canal and pulled myself up onto the algae-covered wooden steps. Lucca managed to control his hysterics just enough to broadcast my spill to every passing gondola driver. "Into the water," he yelled to anyone willing to listen, "like *Baywatch* Pamela Anderson."

Signe bought some beers for Lucca and the other gondola drivers at the station, where Lucca, the human instant replay, began a series of dry-run reenactments of my fall, which he continued for thirty minutes while I dried off, much to the enjoyment of the other gondoliers and a newlywed couple standing nearby.

"In a hundred years," he joked, "come back and we'll be singing about the American who fell into the canal."

"You will?" I asked, falling right into his trap.

"No, the singers will. And you'll have to pay extra to hear it."

Doug Lansky is a nationally-syndicated travel columnist, author of Lonely Planet Signspotting, The Rough Guide First Time to Europe, *and* Last Trout in Venice, *from which this story was excerpted, and editor of the award-winning travel-humor anthology,* There's No Toilet Paper on the Road Less Traveled. *Doug spends most of his time in Europe with his Swedish wife, Signe, a medical doctor, and their young daughters.*

24

GINA BRIEFS-ELGIN

THE CHERUB

Who was that dastardly criminal?

AFTER MY MOTHER'S MEMORIAL MASS, A YOUNG FRIEND confided that my mother had taught her an important life lesson: never serve cantaloupe on an orange-colored plate. I could just hear my mother: "Oh! Not *that* color, dear," my mother would have told her, deftly switching the cantaloupe slices onto Mexican blue glass. "My first thought," said my friend, "was who cares what color the plate is? But later I saw. Your mother taught me that beauty counts. She taught me that it matters how things look."

It mattered to my mother how things looked one drizzly morning on the island of Capri after early Mass. My eighty-five-year-old father had died suddenly in Italy, and my mother, as a distraction from grief, had taken two of my cousins and me on a trip she had originally planned to take with him. My grief was still dormant. The four of us—three giddy girls and my widowed mother—boarded the ferry from the sleazy, criminal docks of Naples and got off on the magical island of Capri, where my mother would commit her own crime. Capri is famous for being one of the most beautiful islands in the world. Travel guidebooks tell me I should remember steep stone streets, whitewashed walls cascading with roses, crimson bougainvillea, yellow broom, and from every viewpoint, the luminous blue sea lying steeply below. An enchanted island! Instead I remember only three brief unenchanted scenes, each I fervently resented then, each my cousins and I love to remember now, thirty years later.

It was early morning. I was trying to keep sleeping, but my mother was violently shaking my foot. She had turned on all the lights in our low-ceilinged hotel room and was dripping water off her raincoat onto my bedclothes.

"Gina! You've got to get up and help me right now. I've done something terrible."

I sat up fast. This pale woman frantically flinging raindrops, her gray hair wild, was so unlike my cheerful and practical British mother—whom lightning, poisonous snakes, and even war had never been able to rattle—that I was alarmed.

"I've done something awful," my mother said, sitting down hard on my feet. "I've stolen something." My heart flopped into my throat—had my father's death unhinged her? She seemed frantic with distress and my mind filled with preposterous thoughts: Had she stolen jewelry? A gun? Had she shot somebody?

I scootched to the foot of the bed. Julie and Tessa and I watched as with shaking hands she opened her straw bag and removed an object hidden under her scarf. "Oh, dear," she said, unveiling the object of her crime. And here it was: a five-inch-high pink plastic dashboard mascot of a roguish little boy. He was holding his outsized dick in his hand and pissing into a little toilet. By means of the handle on the toilet, the penis of this fiendish boy could be ratchetted up or down. Coming out of early morning Mass, glowing with the beauty of the sacrament and the fresh Capri dawn, my mother had stepped into a shop to buy postcards. This hideous toy, grinning at her from the cash register, had struck her like a blow. She had told the shopkeeper it was a shame to have such a thing in such a beautiful setting. She had offered to buy it from him. No, he had said, shrugging, it was a present from a friend. And then he had turned his back. It had taken her only a moment to commit her crime, to swish the ugly thing into her big straw bag and hurry out into the wet street.

> I took the envelope of cash my mother handed me. Perhaps I even looked up *crazy* in the Italian dictionary.

I was outraged and pushed her off my feet. For this she got me up? But my mother was in a frenzy of anxiety.

"What if he saw me?" she says. "What if he told the police? What if it gets into the papers?" She imagined the headlines for us, something like this: "Professor's Widow Steals Obscene Toy." "Gina," she said, "you've got to go right now and explain to that man. Apologize for me."

Now I was scared. Was my mother coming unglued? Why did she have to go and do this crazy thing? And now she wanted me to fix it. But I was proving good at denial these days. "I need more sleep," I told her. "I'll take it back later."

"We're not taking it back," she said. "I just want you to explain to the man and apologize for me. Tell him his island of Capri is so beautiful that he shouldn't have such an ugly thing on his cash register. It doesn't belong. Offer to pay for it." She opened her wallet, her British self again, mustering her troop.

"It doesn't matter what's on a store's cash register," I argued, exasperated now. "It's his store."

"Yes it does," said my mother firmly. "It's ugly and we're not giving it back." She wasn't suffering from madness after all, I realized, just grief and offended aesthetics.

I got resentfully out of the cozy bedclothes. With very bad grace, I took the envelope of cash my mother handed me. Perhaps I even looked up *crazy* in the Italian dictionary. Then I put on my shorts and sweater and stepped out onto the drizzly street. I was aware that I was being a graceless daughter, that Julie or Tessa, who were devoted to my mother, would have embraced the mission of clearing her name. But I was the one who spoke a little Italian. I walked across the cobbles towards the shop, rehearsing my speech, full of dread. And then an idea occurred to me—a way to postpone the moment of walking into the shop. A gesture that might almost redeem me in my own eyes. Minutes ticked by as I ducked in and out of tourist shops, hoping that my cousins were worrying at my delay and not enjoying breakfast without me. At last I lit on another boy-statue, this one a terracotta cherub, genderless, mostly wings.

Armed with my bland cherub, I crossed the street and walked fast into the pillaged shop and straight to the counter before I could lose my courage. But the shopkeeper was talking to a friend, which gave me time to be nervous, time to look at the cash register, where the nasty boy must have been, time to wonder—absurdly—how the shopkeeper could even keep shop, as though nothing had happened, with his interesting mascot missing from right under his eye. Time to wonder whether he knew already the reason that brought me here, while he chatted deliberately on and on.

Finally, the friend moved away from the cash register. I stepped forward, my cherub in hand. I pushed the envelope of lire across the counter, and then I unwrapped the cherub. "This is for you, signor," I told him. "My mother," I said, pointing to the empty spot, "has stolen your boy. She is *matta*, crazy," I told him in broken Italian, dancing my fingers on either side of my face to show him crazy. "My father is dead," I told him.

"*Bene, bene*, it's all right," he told me, mostly bored. But I pressed the modest cherub on him. "*Non, signorina*." He didn't want it and tried to give it back to me.

"Take it!" I said, and fled from the shop. In the drizzly street I cried for a long time, for my father, for my mother, for my unkindness in not recognizing her theft as a symptom of grief. Then I wiped my eyes and went back to the pensione.

On the night we left Capri, my cousins and I leaned over the white ferry railing. The black water was foaming far below us as we ploughed away from the magical island, and we had a job to do. "Here he is!" said Julie. In a moment, she and Tessa were merrily balancing the toy on the railing, pushing the tiny tank handle up and down a last few times. My mother's crime embarrassed me still, and my own unsympathetic heart, but then I was laughing, too, as the three of us, with a giddy hoot, consigned the unzipped boy to the waves.

Gina Briefs-Elgin teaches composition and creative nonfiction at New Mexico Highlands University in Las Vegas, New Mexico. She writes about travel, confectionary, the decorative arts, and the literature of mysticism. Her favorite activities are traveling with her husband and son, riding Amtrak, and fishing trout streams (although it dismays her to catch anything).

25

DAVID FARLEY

THE PASTA NAZI

The menu is just for show.

WITHIN WEEKS OF MOVING TO ROME, JESSIE AND I CONVINCED ourselves we were well on our way to blending in with the locals. Aided by our newly bought, slick shoes, we'd mastered crossing the street (step off the curb with confidence and the traffic will stop); ordering the right coffee at the right time of day (cappuccino in the morning, espresso later); and we spoke enough Italian to get us through most restaurant situations without relying on English.

It didn't take long before our neighborhood, a small patchwork of quiet medieval streets—wedged between the Forum, the Colosseum, and the busy thoroughfare, Via Cavour—felt like a self-contained village. Paulo would throw a slice in the oven for me the second I'd step into the curiously named "Pizza's House"; when I'd blur the pronunciation of *aglio* and *aouli*, the woman at the small vegetable shop around the corner still knew I wanted garlic and not oil, and the lesbians who ran

> "When Italians eat out,
> they expect food just
> like their mama made,"
> a Roman friend told me.
> "Elevating it, like French
> food, would ruin it."

the internet café would play the Indigo Girls for me because I once mentioned I'd seen them in concert back in college. I even started to get used to the instrumental flute versions of Beatles songs played by the Peruvian bard who'd set up near the Forum.

But we weren't prepared for Al Cardello, an eighty-five-year-old eatery that's been run by Angelo and his wife Lidia for as long as anyone can remember. The first time we ate there, it was a warm fall day and Jessie and I took a seat at one of the two white-clothed picnic tables in front. It was half past noon, and, naturally, we were alone—most Romans' stomachs don't begin to growl for at least another hour.

Lidia sauntered out to greet us. After we ordered a liter of the house wine, she asked if we wanted an *antipasto misto*—a starter of mixed grilled vegetables. "Well, perhaps I could see a menu first," I said, stumbling through my newly learned usage of modal verbs in Italian. She nodded her head and stepped back inside. Five minutes later she delivered our wine, but still no menus. We shrugged and poured ourselves a glass.

"*Prego!*" I hollered, when I saw Lidia dart by the doorway. Instead, a large, lumbering man finally emerged.

"So, do you want the *antipasto misto* or what?" said Angelo, wiping his hands on his stained white apron, his voice grumbled and breathy like he'd just trekked up Capitoline Hill to get to us.

"Um...I'm not sure," I said, biting down on my lower lip and sneaking a glance at Jessie.

"It's *buonissimo*," he replied, shaking his hand in front of my

face, his fingers clasped together in that oh-so-Italian hand gesture. "You won't regret it." But before I could consider his offer,
he quickly changed the subject to the main course.

"Today I'm making a delicious seafood fettuccini. You must
have it. It's also *buonissimo*."

"It sounds nice," I said, "but we'd really like to see a menu." I
was actually craving *spaghetti carbonara*, a classic Roman dish made
with eggs and bacon.

"I *could* show you a menu," said the lumbering chef, his gaze
through his thick grease-stained spectacles as strong as a Roman
emperor who had just condemned me to the lions in the nearby
Coliseum, "but I think you should get the seafood fettuccini."

I looked across the table at Jessie and she gave me that look—
lightly shrugging her shoulders, and arching her eyebrows—that
says: we're going to be lion food. And when I turned back, Angelo
had started his descent into the subterranean restaurant. Maybe,
I wishfully thought, he was going to fetch us some menus.

That is, until Lidia emerged with two heaping plates of grilled
vegetables. She was right: the fresh zucchini, eggplant, olives,
green pepper, all slathered in olive oil, really were *buonissimo*. Jessie tossed a slice of eggplant in her mouth and shrugged again:
neither of us actually remembered ordering the *antipasto misto*.

About twenty minutes later, Angelo appeared in front of us
holding two plates of steaming seafood fettuccini. "I guess we're
not going to be getting a menu now," Jessie said, laughing. After
putting the plates down in front of us, Angelo sidled up to two
French tourists, who'd taken the table next to us.

"You must try the seafood fettuccini," Angelo said, pointing
to our food. The couple craned their necks to get a glimpse.

"Yes, that looks nice, but I'd like to see a menu," said the man,
struggling through Italian. Jessie and I smiled at each other, and
sat back to enjoy the inevitable outcome of this battle.

"The seafood is very fresh—it was just delivered."

"That's nice," said the French tourist, "but—"

Angelo interrupted him. "But...but...but," he mimicked the man, pushing the back of his hand closer to the French man's face with every "but," as if he were threatening to slap an unruly child. "You'll have the seafood fettuccini and like it," Angelo announced and stormed into the restaurant. After exchanging *what the ...?* looks, the French couple turned to us. I gave them a sympathetic smile as I twirled some strands of fettuccini with a fork. "Don't worry," I told them. "It's *buonissimo*."

I've been intimidated at restaurants before—usually when I'm eating above my class level: those restaurants that feel so stuffy, you sit for hours in your chair with posture so perfect it makes your back ache afterward. We try to use proper pronunciation, fearing that the mangling of a French menu item or an inappropriate use of "drank" (when we should have used "drunk") will find ourselves lying on the sidewalk before the foie gras arrives. When I lived in Prague, my then-girlfriend and I took a visiting friend to such a place. And when I accidentally screeched my knife across the plate while cutting my fennel-encrusted roast duck stuffed with aioli-marinated foie gras, the fingernails-on-the-chalkboard sound turned my usually relaxed dining companions into schoolmarms. They shushed me—in stereo—temporarily drowning out the classical music. Then they pretended I didn't exist for the rest of the dinner.

But dining in Rome is different. Neither pretentious nor corporate, Roman restaurants boast an atmosphere that's more haphazard than highfalutin: tables are scattered throughout the room as if a blind person had arranged them that evening, menus are often handwritten, and wine is served in glass tumblers. If you feel like you're eating in someone's living room, there's a good reason for it: the strong Italian attachment to family and the fact that the cuisine was more or less born in the home (as opposed to the wealthy royal courts in France), means the ideal meal for an average Roman is one he or she ate growing up. At home. "When Italians eat out, they expect food just like their mama made," a Roman friend told me. "Elevating it, like French food, would ruin it."

So, while sitting on the window sill of our second-story apartment, smoking a roll-up cigarette, and listening to the incongruent Andean sounds of "Let It Be" echo off the cobblestones, I realized that rather than let Angelo's bullying leave a bad taste in my mouth, I needed to readjust the lenses in which I viewed Roman culture. Angelo wasn't a grumpy old chef who cooks what he wants and is prone to backhanding patrons, he was a stern father who knew what was best for my taste buds. And it was only fitting that after a few visits to Al Cardello, Lidia would great us with a hug and refer to herself as our "Roman mama."

Travel comes from the Latin for *travail*, which comes from the word *tripalium*, an instrument of Roman torture. And, evidenced by the word's etymology alone, it's not easy. We can't expect to really get to know a place after three weeks or three months of being there, but we can let the place challenge ourselves, our identities, and our worldview so that when we walk through our front door after a trip we're different people. We're stronger, more open-minded, more tolerant. And maybe, if we're lucky, we've acquired an additional set of parents along the way.

A few weeks and a few more perplexing Al Cardello experiences later, Jessie's parents were in town. When her dad announced he wanted to eat at a *real* Roman restaurant—a place that didn't have tiramisu on the menu, where the waiters didn't start off speaking English, or where there'd be no guidebooks resting on the tables—Jessie and I looked at each other and giggled. I'll be right back, I said, slipping on my shoes, and heading out the door.

Al Cardello wasn't open yet, but the front door was ajar and I could see Angelo sitting at the stainless steel kitchen counter, which faces out to the smaller of the two dining rooms. He was bent over a heaping plate of thick pasta noodles, the steam fogging up his bulletproof glasses, and one of his giant hands wrapped around a half-drunk bottle of white wine. I stepped down into the subterranean restaurant and he grunted an acknowledgment of my presence. When I told him that I needed to make a reservation for four people at nine o'clock that night, he grunted again, and then let his chin fall to his chest, which I took to be an affirmative nod.

Five hours later, we were all seated in Al Cardello's small dining room eyeing the menu (yes, we were actually given a badly Xeroxed menu this time) when Angelo stumbled over to take our orders. I held my breath as Jessie went first.

"I'll have the *spaghetti all' amatriciana*, please."

"O.K.," he said. "And who else is having the *amatriciana*?"

Everyone was silent. We'd all carefully selected different dishes so that we could share.

"*Carbonara*...?" Jessie's dad said.

"No," Angelo barked.

We all paused. No?

"No *carbonara*!" Angelo said.

"Oh, I guess they don't have *carbonara* tonight," Jessie's dad said, quickly running his eyes down the menu for something else to order. "O.K. then, I'd like the lasagna, please," he said, offering the menu in Angelo's direction.

"No!" Angelo said again. "You're all having what she's having," he grunted, pointing to Jessie. "You're all having the *amatriciana*!" Then he walked back into the kitchen.

And somewhere between Jessie's parents exchanging *what the ...?* looks and her dad labeling Angelo "The Pasta Nazi," I mimicked the bad Italian-American voiceover on those Olive Garden commercials: "Al Cardello: when you're here, you're family."

⌒⊘

David Farley is coeditor of Travelers' Tales Prague and the Czech Republic. *His work has appeared in* The Best Travelers' Tales 2004, New York Magazine, Playboy, Condé Nast Traveler, Travel + Leisure, Arthur Frommer's Budget Travel, The Washington Post, *and* Chicago Tribune, *among other publications. He teaches writing at New York University and Gotham Writers' Workshop.*

26

LINDA WATANABE MCFERRIN

ENCHANTED PIAZZA

The sinking city ages but never gets old.

It has been called Europe's grandest drawing room. Capacious and elegant, it is a great circle in which pigeons and people congregate. In winter, the waters rise and fill it. Gondolas slip through it.

It is the Piazza San Marco, center square of Venice, "La Serenissima," that most serene city that kisses the Adriatic Sea. Tonight the Piazza is awash in light. Over it, the full moon hangs like a Venetian glass globe. Ringing its vast perimeter, bandstands sparkle like bejeweled half-shells, cupping dinner-jacketed orchestras and tuxedoed string quartets that fill the night with music. Mozart in one corner. Slow, syrupy jazz in another. Diners dawdle, pick at desserts, savor ports and cognacs and sip at their last espressos.

We stroll through the moonlit piazza. Water colorists vending Venetian scenes sit, with weary smiles, beside their portable stands. Other artists patiently complete the final portraits of the day. The campanile, the Piazza's famous bell-tower, chimes the hour. A clock tower across the square responds—its medieval mechanical figures striking a tinny midnight. The smattering of ambient humanity stops, looks up and smiles before moving on. Artists roll up their drawings and collect their pigments. Musicians put away their instruments. The restaurants grudgingly close.

It is at the Piazetta, vestibule to the Piazza San Marco, that our feet first touch Venetian soil. Disgorged by the fuming *vaporetti*, water buses that ply the Grand Canal, we have entered the city on a carpet of blue. Around us Venice gleams—bone-white—a relic tottering upon its millions of wooden pilings. Great facades, like old courtiers, crack-toothed and leering through years of paint, line the waterways. Venice is a merchant city, its heart perennially set upon the riches of the East. In the sixteenth century it was the largest empire in the West, controlling Crete, Corfu, and the Dalmation Coast. Its arsenal could turn out a fighting galley in a single day. The breeze was one of piracy and larceny. Even the city's patron saint was shanghaied. In 829, Venetian buccaneers stole the bones of Saint Mark the Evangelist from his tomb in Alexandria, smuggling their booty back to Venice in a casket of pork. In 1204, Venice sacked the holy city of Constantinople, confounding its Christian partners on the Fourth Crusade. But Venice is also a place of dreams and mystery, home to adventurers and bon vivants like Casanova and Marco Polo, a giddy world of glass and masks.

We roam the Rialto in the early morning hours, linger on bridges, sip chianti canal-side, slip through the labyrinth of narrow streets to explore shops crammed with precious pieces of Murano glass, fine-blown from spidery filaments, or webs of Burano lace. But mainly we are drawn to shop after shop of papier-mâche masks. Maskers were the popular medieval and Renaissance cel-

> As if in spite, the boats remain a mourning black—
> a dark joke in this city of dark humors. It is this secret
> shadow side that contrasts so seductively with
> the carnival brilliance of Venice.

ebrants and Carnevale was the Venetians' favorite masquerade. The faces of commedia dell'arte characters—Harlequins (colorful clowns), Punchinellos (quarrelsome hunchbacks), and Pierrots (sad-visaged mimes)—grimace on walls alongside beasts and sun kings. The funereal guises of La Buatta, the Domino, with its black cape, white mask, and three-cornered hat, and the black mask and cape of Il Dottore suggest the sinister side of revelry.

Under evening's dusky cloak we glide through the canals in gondolas, the long thin black lacquer boats. Bats (the *pipistrelli*) crisscross the air space over the canals. Our gondolier, Paulo, is quiet and mysterious—pale hair, pale face, vermilion lips bright as the ribbon of his hat. The gondolas remind us of coffins, not surprisingly, for during the Black Plague of the Middle Ages, the Venetians painted their boats black, thinking the bright colors far too festive. As if in spite, the boats remain a mourning black—a dark joke in this city of dark humors.

It is this secret shadow side that contrasts so seductively with the carnival brilliance of Venice. During Carnevale, Venice becomes a madhouse, the Piazza flooded again, this time with revelry. In the weeks before Lent, winter's final grim gauntlet, costumed celebrants fill the Venetian streets. Maskers surge into the ice-bright squares. In recent years the count of partygoers has climbed to over 100,000 people. The cramped streets and bridges swell with them. They spill into the Piazza. In Venice all streets seem to flow into the Piazza San Marco, just as all roads once led to Rome. The parade is Felliniesque—sometimes a breathtaking vision, sometimes a hilarious nightmare—and the cast international. The exotic East sweeps onto the scene in a flurry of capes, turbans, scimitars, and curly-toed shoes. Party-crazed, profiling visitors mingle with the wise and wary Venetians. Plumes, hoods, and tri-cornered hats bob atop the seas of guests that crowd hotel lobbies. Greasepaint, crystal beads, and silk glint and flare in the candlelight of the city's restaurants. Phantoms veiled in tulle or wrapped in clouds of netting disappear around alleyway corners and reappear in neighboring squares.

But there is nothing more haunting than the sight of costumed celebrants ferried through the inky waters by a Charon-like boatman to the lip of another realm. During Carnevale to step into a costume, you remove the one you are wearing. The city is peopled with creatures of the interior landscape—the dreamy, the dangerous, and the archetypal.

This year Carnevale will be observed for nearly a month, but the celebration is such a part of the Venetian soul that in years past Carnevale lasted up to six months. Certainly, in those tiny shops selling masks, the carousel never stops. An atmosphere of transgression and excitement drapes Venice year-round. It is present in strangers who share gondolas, and dinner, and then disappear; in restaurants like the Bai Barbacani—where the titillating conversations between guest and proprietor begin with a plate of plump gnocchi pillows, stained in cuttlefish ink, and an invitation to come into the kitchen, and end in breathless promises to "make marscapone together."

Our hidden and forbidden selves are reflected around us, as in the fractured glass of a fun house mirror, on the walls covered with hundreds of carnival masks. We muse over those masks as we walk in silence along the Riva degli Schiavoni after midnight, just beyond the Piazza San Marco, where canal waters lap hypnotically like a subvocal command. We cannot leave Venice without one. Before we abandon the city, we must rush back to the shops to search for our favorites, seeking to take home with us a cherished touchstone to our secret selves, the lasting symbol of our enchantment.

⌒

Linda Watanabe McFerrin has been traveling since she was two and writing about it since she was six. She is a poet, travel writer, and novelist, who has contributed to numerous publications including the San Francisco Chronicle Magazine, The Washington Post, Modern Bride, Travelers' Tales, *and Salon.com. She is the author of the novel* Namako: Sea Cucumber, *and the short story collection,* The Hand of Buddha. *She is a winner of the Katherine Anne Porter Prize for Fiction, and lives in Oakland, California.*

27

MARY TOLARO NOYES

THE GIFT

The exchange began long before the purchase.

I PUSHED OPEN THE HEAVY WOODEN DOOR OF ORPHEUS AND entered into a small shop overflowing with university students, racks of sheet music, and ancient instruments. Guitars, violins, and even a drum from Africa and a wooden flute from South America hung from floor to ceiling and covered every inch of wall space. The large display window had caught my attention as I wandered in the narrow, porticoed streets of Bologna's university district. My first reaction was to wait for a quieter time, but I would be leaving for home in a couple of days and I still had to buy my son the gift he had requested. Orpheus seemed the perfect place.

A gentleman approached me immediately, in spite of the chaos. He was in his early forties, short, with black hair and thick, dark-rimmed glasses. His large doe-eyes smiled in welcome, as he asked, "*Prego, signora*, can I assist you?"

"*Si, signore, grazie*," I responded. "I'm looking for a gift for my son, who is a musician and requested an alto recorder. I see you have a number of recorders here in the display," and I turned to the glass cabinet to my right, "but I can't distinguish an alto from a soprano!"

"*Benissimo*," he said, his eyes animated all at once. "It would please me to assist you. You see, the alto recorder is my specialty. I teach students from the university and I play in a small professional ensemble." Unlocking the cabinet, he continued, "Please tell me about your son. What is his name?"

"Philip," I replied, and then described him to the professor, his musical experience and his personality: a young man of eighteen, talented, whose soul the world glimpsed when he played thin, lilting melodies on his soprano recorder, or on his flutes and pipes from around the world.

He shook his head slowly as he closed the display and earnestly explained, "*Signora*, these instruments will not satisfy your son's needs. I'm sorry. They are for people without serious intention, or perhaps for beginners. Do you have some time you can spend here, while I demonstrate my meaning?"

"Yes, of course. I would appreciate your assistance, *professore*."

With that he led me out of the tiny, crowded room, through the store's snakelike slither, deep into its chambers, back through a room dedicated to lutes and stringed instruments that hung on the dark walls, back, back, into another recess full of flutes, recorders, oboes, and clarinets. He motioned me to a comfortable, overstuffed chair. I sat down, already half enchanted, while he instructed his young assistant to run next door to the bar and get us each a *caffè*.

In the meantime, he selected seven alto recorders, all made of wood, each a different shade of rich brown. He lined them up on a small, round, mahogany parlor table and described the wood of each instrument, its characteristic sound and special qualities. As he talked, his hands gently caressed the smooth surface of the recorder he held, while his twinkling eyes communicated pleasure.

When the young woman arrived with our *caffè*, he thanked her, encouraged her to join us, and proceeded to entertain with strains of Bach, Vivaldi, and Mozart to demonstrate the particularities of each instrument. Encouraging me to choose the one or two most appropriate for my son's musical style, he exclaimed "*Brava, signora*," pleased when I tentatively made my selections. "You have a good ear. You have chosen well, and now I will help you make the final selection!"

I said "*Professore,* I cannot decide. The beauty of the music confounds me. They are both eloquent. Please help me?"

With that, he immediately segued into what seemed Renaissance court music, demonstrating not only the instrument's vibrancy, but also his own talent and delight in playing. I felt like a guest in the professor's living room, the private concert a gift from the musician's soul. Thoughts of Orpheus, the magic flautist, flitted through my mind as his music filled the resonant space.

I admitted after he had finished that I could not distinguish between the two. I said "*Professore*, I cannot decide. The beauty of the music confounds me. They are both eloquent. Please help me?"

"You are correct," he responded with deference, "they are both truly fine instruments. I understand your confusion. But I will play them each again, and explain the sound and help you decide. Relax for a moment more, please, *signora*."

I listened while he played. In the end logic did not help me decide. I chose one over the other only because its rich tones pulled at me more strongly. Its wood was golden and polished smooth. Fine detailed bands were etched around the ends of each tightly fitting section. Subtle hues of the chestnut grain glowed from deep inside. When I held it, I could feel the warmth of the wood. I imagined Philip with it in his hands, lying on his bed at home, he too serenading me with delight.

We returned to the front of the store and continued our conversation as I paid for the gift. The professor, animated and content, explained the proper care of the recorder, and packaged it for the long trip to California. I assured him as we parted, clasping extended hands warmly, that yes, I would encourage my son to someday make a pilgrimage to Bologna and the music store Orpheus. Then the professor could know him and perhaps they would share a moment of music. I thanked him for his help and he waved as I closed the door behind me.

I exited onto the narrow sidewalk, the darkness creeping slowly into the medieval streets. I hurried on Via Marsala toward Piazza Rossini and home, the professor's music still echoing inside my head. As I crossed the piazza and reached tiny Via Benedetto XIV, my ears caught strains of music on the air, wafting from the inner space of the old city block to my left. The students from the nearby music conservatory were practicing. I changed my focus from the music still resonating in my consciousness to the concert floating around me.

Suddenly the peal of nearby San Giacomo Maggiore's giant bells drowned out the students' practicing. *Dong | dong | dong | dong.* The powerful sound reverberated in the stone streets and under the portico. As I turned left onto Via San Vitale, the bell towers from Bologna's dozens of churches joined in the chorus. I knew the music of its bells would serenade the city for fifteen minutes. It was an evening ritual I had come to savor.

Their joyful pealing reminded me of the treasures I always found in Bologna: the hidden, seductive charm of her streets and her people. I unlocked the heavy, dark, wooden *portone* of the *palazzo* and went in. It slammed shut behind me, but the music accompanied me up the stairs and into my life.

Mary Tolaro Noyes was raised in Bellows Falls, Vermont, where her Sicilian grandparents settled in the early twentieth century. She now lives in San Francisco, California with her husband of thirty-six years, Tom. After years dedicated to teaching and to raising two sons, she has finally come to the writing she always meant to do. Her favorite tales involve chance encounters with people who help her understand their world—and herself. Inspired by rediscovering her grandparents' family in Sicily in 1989, she first visited Bologna in 1994 as a student of Italian. After frequent extended stays there, she has come to regard the Città Rossa as her second home and is still taken by the city's medieval magic and modern charm.

28

CLARE FLEISHMAN

BLESSED WATER

It's the key to civilization.

A TINY LAKE WELLED UP FROM AN INACTIVE VOLCANO, LAGO Martignano was only a thirty-minute drive from Rome yet off the beaten path enough that some native Romans hadn't heard of it. It was a slow hike down over the teeth of the volcano, past horses, dogs, and even some children in strollers; the steep, dusty walk kept the stiletto-heeled crowd away. Down at the lake's edge, a trampoline, swings, and sliding boards poked up from the shallow water while sailboats and paddleboats skimmed the horizon, a few stopping at the opposite shore where a knot of sheep nibbled on underbrush. Those summer days were some of the best of my Italy: horses galloped through the open fields behind me, children somersaulted high above trampolines in the still waters, naked toddlers searched for pretty pebbles, thick-haired boys headed Umbro balls, laughing women played paddleball, old men shared Peroni and stories at the aluminum bar, and bare-breasted couples on double swings nuzzled necks. Life was good.

Italians, most people would agree, know how to relax.

It was always this way.

A mere 3,000 years ago, Etruscans were lolling in hot springs bubbling out of the hills 100 miles north of Lago Martignano. The Romans booted them out—no one knows where the Etruscans went but then no one is sure where they came from either—and steamy orgies were the rage until popes down around the thirteenth century made the baths respectable again.

Three millennia later, the outdoor baths at Saturnia are still a startling sight: Dense clouds of white steam hover over shallow layers of pool after pool of thick Kryptonite-colored water; lumpy shapes in terry bathrobes and plastic sandals dip a toe and

Our children, wanting no part of this bacchanalia, stood by with the dogs. But then when they saw we weren't coming out, maybe even lost forever to some circle of this liquid inferno, they waded in.

then slide, stumble and fall into the simmering waters; young men with smooth chests and girls with flowing hair wade in with gusto, anxious to submerge wet boxers and flimsy underwear beneath the gaze of the admiring. All seem happy to leave their stresses back with the heaping piles of shoes and clothes clotting the rocky bank. Only the dogs look less than relaxed as they watch their masters sink, and stink, for hours in the green phosphoric waters, a piping hot primordial minestrone.

But evolution has its own rewards. Come nightfall, a party atmosphere kicks in at the baths. Enterprising Senegalese men lay out blankets thick with timeless beaded jewelry and for the post-modern—D&G knock-off handbags. A curtain of steam rises like cigarette smoke in a bar, couples float among the bubbles, sleek bodies press together like seals in a slow dance and sausage hors d'oeuvres are served up from grills teetering on rocks. My husband and I jumped in. Our children, wanting no part of this bacchanalia, stood by with the dogs. But then when they saw we weren't coming out, maybe even lost forever to some circle of this liquid inferno, they waded in.

All around Italy elaborate spas and hotels are built around the natural hot springs. Bars, restaurants, fresh water pools, water bars, gyms, massage rooms, and television lounges round out the experience. Health insurance in Italy pays for trips to spas. Backache? *Non problema*, go directly to the spa. Many prescriptions allow a two-week stay.

We preferred a "spur of the moment, pull off the *autostrada*, peel down to your bathing suit, and dip in the hot springs" experience. We most often went to the pools of Viterbo, called the Bullicame, several hundred yards down the road from the fancy Terme dei Papi. Bullicame refers to the volcanic sources in Dante's Inferno—it is the pool of boiling blood into which Guy de Monfort, murderer of the Earl of Cornwall in a church nearby, was immersed up to his neck. Here at the Bullicame, old men in nylon bikinis slather their slack-skinned carotene limbs with pea-green clay scooped from the floor of the pools. Soccer buzzes from a radio set up on the ledge. One man spent the entire afternoon we were there scraping and digging a new basin below the other five; every ten minutes, he took a time-out with a soak.

Starting with a toe, I tested the waters like Goldilocks moving from boiling to very hot to just-right. Aah, that's hot. After fifteen minutes, my body burned lobster red. I would have yelped if I hadn't been so happy. From my wet berth, I could see many miles across overgrown fields danced with poppies and celosia. The sky was wide and a purple smudge of a mountain slept against the horizon. A car in the distance sounded like a kid screwing up his mouth making engine noises. The radio announcer chattered on about Totti and Vieri, the familiar Saturday stew of sports scores and bad calls and Hallelujah choruses. I really should have thought about getting out, but I could not move. Maybe happiness is no more complicated than a nice, hot bath.

While melting in this Prozac cocktail, it crossed my mind that we should shop for real estate in the area. Just a little place close enough for a daily dip. The Viterbo job market didn't look too robust, though. Anyway, time to go. Out on the road by the car we shielded ourselves with beach towels to climb into dry clothes. Only one car honked. No one cares—this is Italy.

After a long soak, it's hard to drive the thirty minutes back to Rome without falling asleep. The best thing to do is to drop into Viterbo, a medieval town that doubles as the induction point for the Italian military. Enjoy the old quarter with its ancient towers and porticos, as well as a tall glass of *café freddo*. The charred oils of dark Arabica coffee beans blend with the sting of sulfur and sweat—a scent so strong it has burned stigmata on the air of Viterbo. But the people living in Viterbo don't smell it. They live with it. We can't see our own faces sprouting wrinkles or our own children growing up. The boy becoming a soldier, Ricin replacing the sword, ape becoming man or even man becoming apelike again—we don't notice any of it. What makes us human—adapting so well to a change in environment—can bury the truth. Man becoming God. That one hides especially well.

Whoa, the coffee must be *very* strong in Viterbo.

Once on a return trip from the baths north of Rome, I stopped in Sovana, a gem of a hill town unknown to tourists. Not a lake, river, or sea touch it, yet tiny Sovana again reminded me of the power of water. Before the Romans, Etruscans inhabited Sovana; their lavish burial grounds still tunnel beneath the village. But the town's celebrity resides in their native son, Pope Gregory VII whose birthplace is marked by a plaque at 47 Via di Mezzo. Never mind that it now houses a Land Snails Museum, which has culled more than three thousand specimens from lakes and ponds from all over the world.

Not one but two churches serve this town of only 100 residents. The large duomo of Saints Peter and Paul at the far end of town boasts intricate Lombard-Romanesque carvings. At the other end of town—several blocks down a cobbled alley—lies Santa Maria with its dull façade. But inside rests a magnificent ciborium, a lavishly-carved canopy created before the ninth century. While we were poking around inside, a new baby in flowing white satin and lacy bonnet was being baptized.

"*Deus et nominee...*" the priest welcomed the baby into a dutiful life of grace with a ladle of cold water. The baby howled, the parents beamed and the priest at the other church worried. The family and friends of the 101st Sovana-ite ("the future" they chuckled to each afterward at the party that would continue until the last person fell asleep) filed out from the tiny church.

Lined and crooked, smooth and straight, all fingers dipped inside marble basins filled with holy water. Some barely touched a drop, not wanting to stain a white linen Sunday suit while others thrust three fingers deep in the bowl, intent on doing it right, like every other rule the Church had handed them since they themselves were baptized. Some of the young ones licked their fingers, thirsty after such a long service. Then before stepping out into the midday sun, each made the Sign of the Cross, dabbing the water on head, chest, and arms. Blessed water.

Clare Fleishman lives in Berlin, Germany where she swims in the refreshing— meaning cold—waters of the many lakes and seas. This is an excerpt from her upcoming book, Saints and Soccer Balls: Seasons in Italy.

29

WENDELL RICKETTS

MANI DI VELLUTO

"Velvet hands" sounds so much better than "pickpocket."

I LOST TRACK OF THE NUMBER OF TIMES I HEARD AN ACCORDI-onist play "My Way" while I was in Rome, but it must have been at least a dozen: a couple of times a day for nearly a week, virtually every time I boarded the Met-ro or the sleek, dark-green light-rail trams that stop just outside Porta del Popolo, the monumental gate designed by Vignola on one face and, on the other, by Bernini a hundred years later, and just down from the ostentatious entrance to Villa Borghese.

The public-transit entertainer seems to be the new wave—new, at least, to me—of Roman panhandling, no casual concept in a city that takes public begging very se-riously. Here, panhandlers kneel, their cups held up and their heads bent, eyes on the ground. You see them on the sidewalks or along the Metro's underground snarl of corridors and stairways. At Porta Portese, the immense public flea market that stretches for something like a kilometer on Sunday mornings along via Portese in the Trastevere, they simply stop in the middle of a literal flood tide of humanity, put down a pillow or sometimes just a scrap of cardboard, and assume the posture. The flood parts, reforming on the other side like whitewater around an upthrust of rock.

Porta Portese was a hoot, the crowd immense, thrumming, absolutely daunting.

As humiliating as such supplication must surely be, not to speak of the physical discomfort, there's a smaller, more private humiliation that comes from observing these rituals of submission. It is wretched by any definition to be forced to beg in order to live, and to witness someone's begging is to be incorporated into a circle of humanity where misery attaches itself to you like a shadow at evening. But when begging is accompanied by a theater—and I use the word in its Artaudian sense—of debasement, of resignation, then the sense of being personally implicated is nearly unbearable.

When Gandhi went to England in 1931 to meet the King, or so the story goes, he wore only a dhoti and told a contemptuous reporter not to be concerned about his lack of clothing, because the King would be wearing enough for both of them. Gandhi's gesture, of course, was chosen with political care, but the semiotics of the two situations are not entirely dissimilar: a near-naked Gandhi at Buckingham Palace mocks the affectations of empire; a bent and menial beggar on an ordinary city street, like something straight out of Dickens, mocks the concept of ordinary comfort.

Rome, meanwhile, remains more infamous for its pickpockets than for its beggars, or perhaps it's simply famous for being infamous. Hand-lettered signs were everywhere in la Metro, pasted onto the walls and the stairway railings, warning of *borseggiatori*.

When I first proposed the trip to the Porta Portese market, the *albergatore* at the bed and breakfast on Piazza Bologna, where I was staying with my friend, Dani, was appalled and immediately set about to talk me out of it. Dani, who hadn't been in Rome for seventeen years, nevertheless joined in enthusiastically. "*È un invito a nozze*," Dani said, pointing to the large, floppy book bag that I insist on carrying everywhere: "That's a wedding invitation."

For his part, the *albergatore* had a story: One day, as he was leaving the bank, he was approached by gypsies asking for money. He gave them a few euro, and then they surrounded him to thank him, kissing his hands and patting his arms. He later discovered that they'd gotten into his pants pocket in the process, making off with 300 euros before he knew what was happening.

Observing that he still hadn't convinced me to abandon Porta Portese, the *signore* launched into other stories, which I'd heard before, about thieves on crowded buses who slash your pockets with surgical scalpels in order to extract the contents, or of others, riding Vespas, who zip up alongside you on the sidewalk, cut the straps of your bag or purse, and disappear into traffic with your valuables.

This, too, is a kind of theater: the telling of the cautionary, not to say the Canterbury, tale. True, what Italians think of as "high crime," even in a huge, chaotic city like Rome, seems relatively tame to an American urban dweller, but still. Passing such stories along has its ritual value, though I have to admit that I remain uncertain what I am supposed to draw from them. Nothing of the kind has ever happened to me in fifteen years of decidedly aleatory travel (knock on wood—or touch iron, as the Italians say), and the only people who've ever taken anything out of my bags or out of my pockets that didn't belong to them have been with the American Border Patrol or the Transportation Security Administration. So what I conclude is: If you're a gypsy and you take from me, that makes you a rat bastard thief, but if you've got a badge and a uniform and you take from me, that makes you one of the good guys.

And people say that the bureaucracy in *Italy* is hard to understand....

In the end, we went to Porta Portese anyway, me and Dani and my wedding invitation. My one concession was to leave my passport at the bed and breakfast—the *albergatore* had a story about that too, which involved an American girl who'd had her passport stolen. She had to spend hours in the Questura and it took days to get a replacement and she missed her plane as a consequence. The one interesting part of the story was that, if you get your passport stolen in Rome, the American Embassy supposedly doesn't make you pay for a new one. I wonder if that's really true.

In addition to the term *borseggiatori*, by the way, pickpockets are also known, much more poetically, as *mani di velluto* (velvet hands).

But to get back to the beginning: The hands that touched the accordion keys were far, far from velvet. The way it works is this. The musician boards, burdened not only by his accordion but also by a small cart on wheels, about the size of the rolla-way bags that people bring onto the airplane because they insist they'll fit into the overhead storage bin, but which then almost always wind up having to be checked from the jetway, which makes everyone testy. Later, the flight attendants come down the aisles to distribute the baggage-claim checks, providing the occasion for someone (and there is always someone) to demand to know whether his bag will "definitely" be waiting for him when he lands, and for the flight attendant to answer cheerfully, "It's on the same plane as you are, sir!"

No one ever says, at that point, "Thanks for making us all late taking off because you were determined not to spend fifteen minutes at baggage claim." No one ever says it, in spite of the fact that the world is full of people who'd rather inconvenience you than risk being inconvenienced, which is no doubt the way The Golden Rule works in hell.

The rolling cart bears a large, boxy speaker and a smaller apparatus on top, which was either a CD or a cassette player (I never got close enough to check), secured by bungee cords. Out of the speaker comes the bass line and the percussion, and the accordionist supplies the melody. Rome is a large and grand place, so it hardly seems possible that every single subway musician had the same karaoke percussion tape (I think that's what they're called), but they all had "My Way," and "My Way" was always the first track. Perhaps it scarcely needs to be said that "My Way," played on the accordion and accompanied by a sort of bossa nova beat, is a pitiful and denatured thing.

Sometimes there was time for a second number—the tape also contains "Ode to Joy" and "March of the Toreadors"—but sometimes it was just an endless loop of "My Way." When the musician decided that we'd had enough, he (and they were always men) came around with a paper cup or once, prosaically, with a hat, to collect money. Here, there was no deference, but rather the vaguely combative expectation that you had received a service and now ought to be willing to pay for it.

I don't know whether this would qualify, under San Francisco's draconian law, as "aggressive panhandling," but it's certainly *pushy*, in the same way that people who talk too loud on cell phones are pushy, taking up more than their share of the space. Too, it's rather a mockery of the fine tradition of the street performer, the busker (a word that comes from Italian, as it happens—from the verb *buscare*, to search for or, in one sense, to procure). But perhaps that's too fine a point to make. Everyone's got to live. At night, the cavernous enormity of Stazione

Termini becomes a bedroom for scores of people who have no place else to go. No one shoos them out.

I should say that Porta Portese was a hoot, the crowd immense, thrumming, absolutely daunting. It wasn't until we got to the end that Dani and I discovered the traditional part of the market, the part that's really a "flea market," where there are fake Roman antiques and dog-eared books and Nazi memorabilia and old, hand-blown bottles and some awfully nice secondhand furniture, really. The rest has become a sort of outdoor mall, with (mostly) crappy wares from everywhere but Italy.

I scandalized Dani by buying a *porchetta*, a roast-pork sandwich, from a vendor and eating it as we walked, but I think what really got to him was that, when they asked if I wanted *maionese*, I said yes.

But then I'm always running afoul of the rules of food in Italy, which are many, various, and capricious. That's one (small) downside of knowing Italians: They always tell you when you're wrong about food. There were disapproving looks when I asked for Coca-Cola with pizza or for a limoncello before supper (it's a *digestivo*, stupid) and discernible gasps one evening in Lecce when I asked the waiter for a cappuccino at the end of supper. One only drinks cappuccino *con colazione* (that is, at breakfast), I was given to understand, because it's bad to consume milk at night. I looked around the table: Francesco was having *panna cotta*, Mimmo had ordered gelato.

"So let me make sure I understand," I said, "you're giving me shit for ordering a cappuccino because you shouldn't drink milk at night, and yet both of you are eating milk products."

They looked down at the dishes in front of them. "*Beh, in effetti, sì….*"

"*Allora va fa'n culo!*" I said, and they—generous, kind-hearted, and more capable than I am of embracing paradox—laughed and laughed until my cappuccino came.

Wendell Ricketts is a writer, editor, poet and playwright. You can view his work at mondowendell.com

SHEILA WRIGHT

THE NATURE OF ITALY

It makes her tremble on many levels.

LIVING IN DENSELY POPULATED SOUTHERN ITALY, I FIND I miss the immense, almost untouched face of the Canadian wilderness. In Naples, shrouds of chaos and human growth cover the natural past. I long to walk for hours in a forest without seeing or hearing another human being. Even where I live, on the Sorrentine Peninsula, not one stone remains unturned. Every possible space has been exploited for growing olives, lemons or grapes. On solitary walks, across seemingly deserted mountains, I hear the shrill cries of a goatherd or the startling report of a gun.

One day, when I'm in the middle of a lesson on phrasal verbs, the classroom tilts. The move is quick, like the gentle nudge of an elevator. There is a split-second of silence before the students all start talking at once, joking nervously and wanting to know my reaction to the earthquake. I am stunned at first, then exhilarated. Yes, exhilarated. The living planet had shifted below me, instantly altering my perspective and connecting me to the infinite cycle of geological creation and destruction.

This region of Italy has had its share of natural disasters. The Sorrentine Peninsula has been spared from the worst, but places less than forty kilometers away like Pompeii and Herculaneum attest to much greater misfortunes. These cities were buried under lava and volcanic ash when Vesuvius erupted in 79 A.D. and have been unearthed over the last few hundred years to reveal a civilization frozen in time.

. . . for how can you argue scientific probabilities with Neapolitans, a people proud to be counted among the contrary believers of the world?

Almost a million people live around the periphery of Mount Vesuvius, despite a government initiative offering large sums of money for relocation. I ask my fiancé, Gino, why people continue to raise families on an active volcano. "Because it's cheap," Gino replies. "The money the government offers may seem like a lot, but property prices elsewhere are so high, it really amounts to a very small percentage of what a family would need to start over. Besides, Vesuvius hasn't erupted in many years. People are forgetting."

I feel there must be more to it, for how can you argue scientific probabilities with Neapolitans, a people proud to be counted among the contrary believers of the world? Flowery offerings grease the palms of saints, or at least their likenesses, installed conveniently into street-side niches like pay phones with a direct line to God. Did a statue of San Gennaro mysteriously topple over in the night? There will be a run on the lottery number 19 because it corresponds to this saint in *La Smorfia*, a guide to lottery numbers and their symbols. 19 doesn't come up? Well, you should have played 1 and 9 separately, since San Gennaro split in two when he hit the ground. There is always a higher power at work. Communicate effectively with this power, divine its methods, and all will be well. Connections are everything.

The power I wish to communicate with lies not only in the heavens, but also under my feet. The earthquake has awakened a primal desire within me. My natural core yearns to experience, at a deeper level, this force that is somehow related to the forests of Canada and yet so different from anything I have known before.

Gino understands my need. One chilly day in February, he takes me to Pozzuoli, just north of Naples, to visit the Solfatara. It is a brimstone-scented place where Mother Earth's heart beats close to the surface, where her breath steams and mud-blood bubbles. I am not entirely afraid since we have paid an admission to enter this no-man's land. It is a natural attraction, like Yosemite's geysers, supposedly safe if you follow the rules and stay away from the roped-off areas.

We have the place to ourselves, and as I step out into the sulphurous valley, I have the strange sensation of walking on another planet while at the same time feeling closer to the Earth than ever before. We are careful not to step in the pools of boiling mud or on the *fumaroli*, holes out of which vapor hisses. "According to legend," says Gino, "this is where the Greeks first conceived their idea of hell." I find the place eerie, but strangely welcoming. A half-ruined Roman sauna beckons to us, and we crouch inside, breathing deeply, letting the thick warmth invade our lungs and bodies. We come out feeling drugged. I crave more.

The next weekend, we continue my quest. A bus takes us part way up Mount Vesuvius, then we walk. The side of the crater is just bare rubble. Nothing grows in this sun-scorched environment and I am glad there is a fresh winter breeze. 1,277 metres above the sea, we have a grand panorama of the Bay. The islands of Procida, Ischia, and Capri rise from the azure expanse like prehistoric sea creatures. We approach the edge of the caldera and peer into the mouth of Vesuvius, a pit full of rocks, steam and garbage. Then we look the other way, down towards Pompeii. Between the crater and the famous ruins, there is just us and a couple of kilometers of volcanic scree. The sun paints our shadows on the vapour, causing our image to shimmer inside the volcano.

Somewhere far below our feet, the Earth's skeleton is contorting: the African plate is slowly pushing itself beneath the Eurasian plate, causing the Mediterranean basin to shrink, Vesuvius to remain active and Pozzuoli to rise. How can we not feel this with our whole being? We stand here insolently, so out of touch with our real beginnings. I shift pebbles of solidified magma under the soles of my shoes. Some trickle down the slope towards distant terraces heavily cultivated with broccoli, anise, citrus fruit and flowers. "Volcanic soil is the most fertile on the planet." says Gino. I'm about to say how ironic it is that such a violent force produces vibrant new life, but then I realize that it has nothing to do with irony. It is simply the way nature works, forever creating and consuming and creating again. I pick up a pebble and hold it in the palm of my hand. It is rough and cool, but I can feel an energy within it that was once sultry and smooth as blood.

The following weekend we take the train to Pompeii. I had already been here during my early days as a culture-blind tourist. Ignoring the modern city, I had made a beeline for the excavations. But now my eyes are opening to the layers of Italy. I see that Pompeii is traffic jams and tramways, language schools and supermarkets, hospitals and banks. And 600,000 people who go about their business, seemingly as oblivious to the threat of Vesuvius as those who lived and died here in 79 A.D.

Gino's sister, Ornella, will be married at Our Lady of Pompeii, a sacred place where pilgrims flock to give thanks for a cure or to pray for benediction. All of Gino's family will be here. And I will attend, struggling in high heels on the cobbled streets, understanding little of the lengthy mass, admiring instead the grand interior of the massive church. How many of us will notice Vesuvius that day? Certainly not Ornella, who will be too busy worrying about the dirt on her hemline and the smooth-running of the impending twelve-course meal. Like most Italian brides, she will have spent the last twelve months shopping, planning and agonizing over each detail. The stress of arguing daily with her mother and future in-laws about such minutiae as whether the marinated clams should be served before or after the grilled octopus will have caused her to lose weight. This wedding is the grand culmination of all that sweat and anguish; Vesuvius is only an afterthought, if that.

Revisiting the excavations, I am drawn, not to the mosaics, temples and shops, but to the suffocated bodies, eerie prostrate forms preserved forever in volcanic ash. Flesh is gone, but a presence remains, laid bare for even the chaos-weary to perceive. What could be a more powerful reminder of nature's enormity?

The following summer, Gino and I make our first snorkelling trip together along the Amalfi coast. The gear is new to me so I follow Gino's lead, cramming my feet into the fins, squashing the mask over my face, wedging the snorkel into my mouth. I am immobilized, literally a fish out of water. I glance at the other beach-goers stretched comfortably on *lettini* provided by a nearby hotel. They watch me, too, from under their *ombrelloni* and designer sunglasses. The Mediterranean is only their backdrop; many of them will never set foot in it.

Once in the shallows, I practice breathing with my face in the water for a minute or two and then we are off, skimming weightlessly out to sea. From Positano we will round the tower-capped headland to a secluded cove. Gino tows a dinghy filled with our towels and a picnic. The sound of my breath in the snorkel unnerves me; it is loud and external, like the rasping of an antiquated life support machine. The water turns from light turquoise to darkest green. I can no longer see the bottom. A looming black shape startles me and I rise up, gasping. I grab the dinghy and rest on its side. Gino stops and we take a break in the sun, admiring the coastline from this new perspective. Positano is postcard perfect, a many tiered mosaic of pastel wash and brilliant tile. Purple, pink and orange paragliders rise from the top of the mountain to coast on warm air before wafting and twirling toward the beach. I float in Mother Earth's rolling belly, terrified to be at the mercy of the sea, but at the same time exhilarated by its immensity and quiet brooding power. Gino loves the sea. "It is the womb from which we were all born," he likes to say. "Returning to it is a wondrous experience."

Rounding the headland we turn towards our cove of the day. We have it completely to ourselves; it is hidden even from the road above. Fallen rocks are strewn on the beach and in the water. During the rainy season, whole sections of the coast crumble into the sea. Today, however, all is sunny and benign as we haul the dinghy ashore. We spread our towels on the coarse sand and bask in the sun, even daring for a while, until a boat passes too close, to shed our swimsuits. We eat part of our picnic, then doze in the shade of the cliff. Afterwards, we explore the *fondali* of the cove, following turquoise and yellow fish that dart into crevasses in the sunken boulders. Delicate sea plants float and dance with the swell. The sun coruscates through the rippling water, making a crazy checkerboard of the sea floor. I bob comfortably now in the shallows, sifting shells and stones through wrinkled mer-fingers. Gino and I play together like dolphins, diving down to the bottom, then with backs arched, arms outstretched, falling slowly up to the surface through aquamarine perfection. Rising to the beach, we let the sea-drops dry on our skin; they are salty, like tears, evaporating quickly in the sun.

We stay until the sun begins to downshift. To the west, the sea cradles tiny stars on the crest of each wave; to the east, turquoise hues deepen and mix with gold, preparing for the onset of indigo that will rise from the deeps before the moon turns on its silvery light. The Maestrale breeze whispers gentle blessings to the sand and rocks, leaving the world peaceful and serene in its wake. A rainbow of blues stretches toward us: from rich sapphire out at sea, each shade becomes slightly lighter until a transparent hue is reached closest to shore. I want to possess these colours, take them home and add them to the forest greens, browns and ochres of my country. Why not? I see now that the true nature of Italy doesn't lie on the surface, in its museums, its cuisine, but rather below and around these things. Canada and Italy and the rest of the world are connected through seas and oceans and molten rock. I am suddenly at home on the planet. Salted with the Earth's minerals, we swim back into the setting sun, exhausted and fulfilled.

⌒ↄ

Sheila Wright taught English in Southern Italy for three years. While she was there she collected, among other things, many fascinating stories and a Neapolitan husband. She now lives in Ontario, Canada, where she is a full-time mother, part-time writer, and the host of the Warkworth Writers' Group. She is currently completing the final draft of her first book, a memoir entitled To Italy with Love, *from which this story is excerpted.*

INDEX

ACKNOWLEDGMENTS

"Burglars in Paradise" by Phil Thompson published with permission from the author. Copyright © 2006 by Phil Thompson.

"Cutouts" by Constance Hale published with permission from the author. Copyright © 2005 by Constance Hale.

"Only Fish" by Bonnie Smetts published with permission from the author. Copyright © 2006 by Bonnie Smetts.

"*Mammone Mio*" by Aimeé Dowl published with permission from the author. Copyright © 2006 by Aimeé Dowl.

"Pieve San Giacomo" by Jason Wilson excerpted from *Grand Tour: The Journal of Travel Literature*. Copyright © 1996 by Jason Wilson. Reprinted by permission of the author.

"The Partisan Artisans of the Oltrarno" by Bill Fink published with permission from the author. Copyright © 2006 by Bill Fink.

"The Synergism of Little Kindnesses" by David Yeadon excerpted from *The Way of the Wanderer* by David Yeadon. Copyright © 2001 by David Yeadon. Reprinted by permission.

"A Cold Day in the Dolomites" by Laura Read published with permission from the author. Copyright © 2006 by Laura Read.

"Under the Tuscan Sky" by Michael Shapiro adapted from *A Sense of Place* by Michael Shapiro. Copyright © 2004 by Michael Shapiro. Reprinted by permission.

"Standing in Line" by Thelma Louise Stiles published with permission from the author. Copyright © 2006 by Thelma Louise Stiles.

"Mirage" by Paola Corso published with permission from the author. Copyright © 2005 by Paola Corso.

"Roman Holiday" by Taras Grescoe reprinted from the July/

ABOUT THE EDITORS

James O'Reilly, president and publisher of Travelers' Tales, was born in England and raised in San Francisco. He graduated from Dartmouth College in 1975 and wrote mystery serials before becoming a travel writer in the early 1980s. He's visited more than forty countries, along the way meditating with monks in Tibet, participating in West African voodoo rituals, living in the French Alps, and hanging out the laundry with nuns in Florence. He travels extensively with his wife, Wenda, and their three daughters. They live in Palo Alto, California, where they also publish art games and books for children at Birdcage Press (www.birdcagepress.com).

Larry Habegger, executive editor of Travelers' Tales, has been writing about travel since 1980. He has visited almost fifty countries and six of the seven continents, traveling from the Arctic to equatorial rainforests, the Himalayas to the Dead Sea. In the early 1980s he co-authored mystery serials for the *San Francisco Examiner* with James O'Reilly, and since 1985 their syndicated column, "World Travel Watch," has appeared in newspapers in five countries and on WorldTravelWatch.com. As series editors of Travelers' Tales, they have worked on more than eighty books, winning many awards for excellence. Habegger regularly teaches the craft of travel writing at workshops and writers' conferences (www.larryhabegger.com), and he lives with his family on Telegraph Hill in San Francisco.

Sean O'Reilly is director of special sales and editor-at-large for Travelers' Tales. He is a former seminarian, stockbroker, and prison instructor who lives in Virginia with his wife Brenda and their six children. He's had a lifelong interest in philosophy, theology, and travel, and recently published the groundbreaking book on men's behavior, *How to Manage Your DICK: Redirect Sexual Energy and Discover Your More Spiritually Enlightened, Evolved Self* (www.dickmanagement.com). His most recent travels took him through China, Thailand, Indonesia, Malaysia, and the South Pacific.

Made in the USA
Charleston, SC
25 August 2010